AS IT WAS
IN THE
BEGINNING

D1531149

AS IT WAS
IN THE
BEGINNING

THE COMING DEMOCRATIZATION
OF THE CATHOLIC CHURCH

———— ✝ ————

ROBERT McCLORY

A Crossroad Book
The Crossroad Publishing Company
New York

BX 1803
.M33
2007

0140104829

The Crossroad Publishing Company
16 Penn Plaza – 481 Eighth Avenue, Suite 1550
New York, NY 10001

Printed in the United States of America on acid-free paper.

The text of this book is set in 10.5/13 Sabon. The display face is Tiepolo.

Library of Congress Cataloging-in-Publication Data

McClory, Robert, 1932-
    As it was in the beginning : the coming democratization of the Catholic
Church / Robert McClory.
      p. cm.
    Includes bibliographical references and index.
    ISBN-13: 978-0-8245-2419-7 (alk. paper)
    ISBN-10: 0-8245-2419-5 (alk. paper)
    1. Catholic Church – Government – History. 2. Laity – Catholic
Church – History. 3. Church renewal – Catholic Church.
4. Democracy – Religious aspects – Catholic Church. I. Title.
BX1803.M33 2007
262'.02 – dc22

                                     2007022599

Contents

Part III
THE FUTURE

Preface and
Acknowledgments

———— ✝ ————

For some, the subtitle of this book may seem audacious, maybe even a cruel joke. When I first suggested it to friends, many looked surprised or incredulous. "Going to be a pretty short book?" said one. Another commented, "I didn't know you were going into fiction."

It's true, of course, that the notions of "democracy" and "Catholicism" do not often appear in the same sentence, much less on the cover of a book. But I don't believe they are as far apart as they seem, either as concepts or as the future of the Catholic Church. Appearances are often deceiving.

I know many Catholics who are profoundly disturbed at the present direction of the institutional church. They observe the growing centralization of its governance, the narrow, often literal interpretation of doctrine, the instinctive rejection of modern culture and the modern world, the vigorous effort to promote outmoded forms of piety. The institution appears to be moving in reverse — back into an older, safer, more protected age. This seems to be the trajectory of the Roman Catholic Church today. I say "appears" and "seems" because I do not believe this represents the future. The present direction is the result of a limited, crippled view of history. And it will pass. The larger view is quite different, and it is this that I attempt to sketch in the book.

From its earliest days, the community founded by Jesus strove to operate in a manner contrary to the style of the Greco-Roman world, contrary, in fact, to that of any previous culture or civilization. Soon, however, some of the unique characteristics of that gospel culture tended to be diminished, given low priority or simply replaced by more worldly, "practical" principles of operation. The shift did not happen all at once, nor did it come about without notice or protest. The history of the church can be understood, I think, as the ongoing effort to restore the church, in some of its essentials, to what it was in the beginning. That is the point of Part I—the Past. I then propose on the basis of the evidence we have today that the church is, if not on the doorstep, at least in the anteroom of that coming restoration. The signs of the times are all around us if we only look. And that is the point of Part II—the Present. Exactly when or how this will come to pass, I can only conjecture briefly in Part III—the Future.

I'm sure some will want to dismiss this as the wishful thinking of a hopeless liberal, still mesmerized by the vision of the Second Vatican Council. And I try to acknowledge in the book where and how my own experience has affected my take. But I have relied largely on the thinking, research, and interpretation of respected scholars and journalists throughout the work. They are the large minds who have mined the sources and who provide the foundation for my argument. Believing in the ongoing, ever surprising presence of the Holy Spirit in the church, I merely attempt to point to what has been lost and to what we are about to find.

I wish to thank those who aided and abetted me in this project and who provided encouragement. I am especially grateful to Jeremy Langford, who believed in the concept from the beginning and who cut through numerous entanglements to make it happen. I also appreciate the calm support and patience of Crossroad editor John Jones. I am most thankful to long-time friend and ecclesiologist George Hinger, who supplied me with ideas, insights, and an enormous amount of relevant literature with the salient points handily pre-underlined, and to Richard Gaillardetz, who said the project was both interesting and possible. Thanks also go to Meinrad Scherer-Emunds and the staff at *U.S. Catholic* magazine; to the stimulating breakfast group at the Heartland Cafe, especially Bob Heineman, Richard

Adams, Lawrence McCarthy, and Jeff Shepard; to Bob and Rosemary Keller; to Sister Wendy Cotter, C.S.J.; to Bob Dugan; and to the staff of the United Library of Garrett-Evangelical and Seabury-Western Theological Schools. Generous assistance, suggestions, and critique were supplied by my daughter, Jennifer, who showed me how to write the book. My largest debt of gratitude is to my wife, Margaret, who served as wise counselor, constant inspiration, gentle critic, and tireless preliminary editor of every word.

Introduction

The Great Temptation

———— ✝ ————

The absolute and immutable truth preached by the apostles from the beginning may never be believed to be different, may never be understood in any other way.
— POPE PIUS X, Oath Against Modernism

MANY YEARS AGO when I was a theology student in a major seminary, I read Dostoyevsky's novel *The Brothers Karamazov*. We were not supposed to read novels because it was feared they would distract us from our studies. We had no access to television, radio, or secular newspapers for the same reason. We were not permitted to have visitors in our rooms or to allow another seminarian into the room at any time. We observed the Great Silence from 9:30 at night until after meditation and Mass the next morning. During the school year we enjoyed one two-week vacation at our homes during the bleakest period of winter, the last week of January and the first week of February.

The seminarians found various ways to maintain sanity in this monastic environment, some by smuggling in newspapers or magazines, some by hurling themselves into breakneck sports during brief recreation periods, still others by contracting mysterious, chronic ailments that required visits to doctors in the city every two weeks.

I read a lot of history books in the library and often gazed longingly at the third floor in the old building. There, behind a locked wrought-iron gate was a large section that housed the works on the Church Index of Forbidden Books, including the

1

writings of heretics, Jews, atheists, agnostics, non-Christians, suspect Catholic theologians, and of course — novelists. By tradition, everyone referred to this section as "hell."

However, the library basement housed a substantial collection of non-circulating reference books, and among them was a beautifully bound set of the University of Chicago's Great Books. Yielding to youthful temptation, I began to unobtrusively borrow a volume every so often, hiding each under the bulky, hooded overcoat we wore and smuggling it out of the library undetected. One of the first was *The Brothers,* about which I knew little at the time. Yet in the sepulchral quiet of my room I was transfixed for the next week by this nine-hundred-page volume — a combination murder mystery, love story, critique of religion, and synthesis of Russian spirituality. It was both riveting and terrifying to me at the time. I have read few books like it since. But nothing in *The Brothers* was quite so provocative as a chapter called "The Grand Inquisitor."[1]

Perhaps that was because I was beginning to reflect seriously for the first time on why I had chosen to place myself in this austere place, or maybe it was just because there was little in the classroom, the textbooks, or the spiritual routine that seemed to stimulate the imagination. The "Grand Inquisitor" stayed on my mind, with its stark charges against the Roman Catholic Church I was preparing to serve — charges that were fantastic and incredible, yet seemed to contain troubling grains of truth.

In the story, Ivan, the cynical, rebellious Karamazov brother, presents to Alyosha, his idealistic, mystical sibling, the outline of an epic poem he would like to write. The plot, he explains, is set in sixteenth-century Seville, Spain, at the height of the Inquisition. Suddenly without fanfare, Jesus appears and walks among the people as he once did centuries before. Everyone immediately recognizes him. They are drawn to him and crowd around as he blesses them. He heals with a touch a man born blind and raises to life a dead girl whose body is being carried into the cathedral. Children cry out in amazement, "It is he! It is he!"

Watching these wondrous events is a cardinal, the Grand Inquisitor himself. He is, says Ivan, ninety years old, "tall and erect, with a withered face and sunken eyes in which there is still a gleam of light." He raises a finger, bidding his guards to take this man prisoner, and such is the cardinal's power that the crowd makes room so the guards can pass through and lead Jesus away. That night the cardinal, carrying a lamp, enters the dungeon where the prisoner awaits. "Is it Thou, Thou?" he asks, but receiving no answer, he adds at once, "Don't answer, be silent. What canst Thou say indeed?"

He then begins a long, accusatory monologue, which is the center of Ivan's poem. "Why hast Thou come to hinder us?" he asks. "For Thou hast come to hinder us and Thou knowest that." The cardinal threatens to burn Jesus at the stake the next day, adding, "The very people who kissed Thy feet, tomorrow at the faintest sign from me will rush to heap up the embers of the fire."

The old inquisitor's complaint is basically this: that Jesus refused to use his power to relieve mankind of the burden of freedom. Freedom of faith "was dearer to Thee than anything in those days fifteen hundred years ago," he says. "Didst Thou not often say, 'I will make you free'? But now Thou hast seen these 'free men.'... Yes, we've paid dearly for it... *but at last we have completed that work in Thy name.* For fifteen centuries we have been wrestling with Thy freedom but now it is over and ended for good."

Why, the inquisitor wants to know, did not Jesus follow the advice of the spirit which tempted him in the desert, "the wise and dread spirit, the spirit of self-destruction and non-existence?" If only Jesus had listened and turned stones into bread, humankind would have run after him like a flock of sheep. "But Thou wouldst not deprive man of freedom and didst reject the offer, thinking, what is that freedom worth, if obedience is bought with bread?" The rejection was a terrible mistake, he declares; humanity cannot tolerate the gift of freedom, because humans are "weak, vicious, worthless and rebellious." And so, they turn to the few who dare to lead. "They will marvel at us and look on us as gods, because we are ready to endure the freedom which they have found so dreadful, and to rule over them."

Choosing bread, he says, Jesus would have satisfied the universal need of humanity to find someone to worship and to find something that all would believe in and worship together. "This craving for community of worship is the chief misery of every man individually and of all humanity from the beginning of time," he says. "For the sake of common worship they've slain each other with the sword.... And behold, instead of giving a firm foundation and setting the conscience of man at rest forever, Thou didst choose all that is exceptional, vague and enigmatic; Thou didst choose what is utterly beyond the strength of man."

The inquisitor and his colleagues have seen enough of pathetic human failure. "We have corrected Thy work," he says, "and have founded it upon miracle, mystery and authority." And humanity rejoices "that the terrible gift that brought them such suffering was at last lifted from their hearts."

He then reveals part of the "mystery" that drives those who control the church: "Listen then. We are not working with Thee, but with *him* — that is our mystery. It's long — eight centuries — since we have been on *his* side and not on Thine. Just eight centuries ago, we took from him what Thou didst reject with scorn, that last gift he offered Thee, showing Thee all the kingdoms of the earth. We took from him Rome and the sword of Caesar, and proclaimed ourselves sole rulers of the earth."

The work is not completed yet, the old man acknowledges, though the movement is well on its way. "They will adore as their saviors those who have taken on themselves their sins before God. And they will have no secrets from us. We shall allow or forbid them to live with their wives and mistresses, to have or not to have children...and they will submit to us gladly and cheerfully. The most painful secrets of their consciences, all, all they will bring to us and we shall have an answer for all.... All will be happy, all the millions of creatures except the hundred thousand who rule over them. For only we, we who guard the mystery, shall be unhappy. There will be thousands of millions of happy babes, and a hundred thousand sufferers who have taken upon themselves the curse of the knowledge of good and evil. Peacefully they will die, peacefully they will expire in Thy name, and beyond the grave they will find nothing but death. But we shall keep the secret, and for their happiness we shall allure them with the reward of heaven and eternity."

Ivan's brother, Alyosha, who has been listening intently, can contain himself no longer. "But...that's absurd," he cries. "Your poem is in praise of Jesus, not in blame of Him — as you meant it to be. And who will believe you about freedom? Is that the way you understand it?" It's certainly not the idea of the Orthodox Church, he says, and if there's some such control conspiracy at all, it might be found in certain quarters of the Roman Church or among some of the Jesuits. Church claims of sovereignty and power come from a "simple lust of power, of filthy gain, of domination," he says, "something like a universal serfdom with them as masters."

Ivan urges his brother to calm down. If Alyosha regards it as fantasy, "let it be so." Still, he says, is it not possible that there have been some, like the old inquisitor, who loved the poor masses that will never be able to measure up or ever be able to use their freedom constructively? "Who knows," he says, "perhaps the spirit of that accursed old man who loves mankind so obstinately in his own way is to be found even now in a whole multitude of such old men, existing not by chance but by agreement, as a secret league formed long ago for the guarding of the mystery, to guard it from the weak and the unhappy, so as to make them happy."

What mysteries, what secrets? protests Alyosha. "Perhaps [this is] nothing but atheism, that's all their secret. Your inquisitor does not believe in God, that's his secret!"

"What if it is so," says Ivan. "At last you have guessed it. It's perfectly true that that's the whole secret."

Alyosha stammers on while Ivan finishes his tale: When the inquisitor stopped talking, he waited for the prisoner to reply, but he merely looked gently at the face of his accuser. "The old man longed for him to say something, however bitter and terrible. But He suddenly approached the old man in silence and softly kissed him on his bloodless lips. That was all his answer. The old man shuddered. His lips moved. He went to the door, opened it and said to him: 'Go and come no more...come not at all, never, never!' And he let Him out into the dark alleys of the town. The Prisoner went away."

A Tinge of Queasiness

At the time I read the story, I was unable to state clearly why it simultaneously frightened and fascinated me. I identified with Alyosha's skepticism, rejecting as ridiculous the idea of a secret coterie of committed atheists overseeing the church out of pity for hopeless humanity. But in moments of weakness, I fantasized that on the eve of my ordination to the priesthood, a knock might come at my door and the rector of the seminary would enter and say, "My son, you and a few others have been chosen to join the hundred thousand, to know the terrible secret that we have carefully guarded. If you wish to hear it and swear never to reveal it to the outside world, I will speak it to you. If not, then I will leave immediately, and God bless you." What would I have said?

As it turned out, during the remaining years of studying theology no one ever revealed a secret to me about anything, and so my faith both in the existence of God and the forthright intentions of the church remained relatively firm. Still, the wizened old inquisitor had left with me a kind of skepticism, a tendency to see discrepancies between what teachers and superiors said and what they really meant.

In the seminary we were being trained in the truth that would make us free, yet rarely did we ever engage in discussion or wrestle with the implications of what we were learning, or better, memorizing. In the one-semester history of philosophy class, for example, we took on all the important philosophers of the ages, from Socrates to Sartre, two or three of them per class. We'd hear about their views, quickly discover how wrong and out of touch with the Catholic Church they were, and move on. Only one philosopher had all the answers, and that was the thirteenth-century genius and saint, Thomas Aquinas.

The study of theology was almost exclusively Thomistic, with supportive reliance on short quotes from Scripture (both Old and New Testaments) used to buttress arguments or refute nonbelievers. Context did not seem important. What was required was the telling reference or the decisive declaration of the appropriate ecumenical council. The study of Scripture itself had not yet emerged from Catholic hibernation, so questions were answered and doubts assuaged by the supreme authority of the Vatican's Biblical Commission, which ruled, among other things, that the Torah, the first five books of the Bible, were personally written by Moses. How they knew this to be so, we were not informed. Rome had spoken; the matter was settled.

When it came time to produce a written thesis for my theology degree, I asked to explore the notion of divine revelation as understood by the Catholic Church in contrast to its understanding by Protestant thinkers Rudolf Bultmann and Paul Tillich. My idea was approved, but I was told I would have no access to any books or articles by the Protestants I was studying. The gates of "hell" would remain firmly locked. The solution was to read Catholic authors, find what they had to say about Protestant ideas of revelation, glean a few quotes of the Protestant writers as cited in the approved sources, and then try to stitch together something that made sense. The effort was somewhat frustrating, like trying to interview someone by quoting what other people said about him. But it was accepted by my theology professor, an aged Jesuit, who, I suspected, had not read anything by Bultmann or Tillich either.

Spiritual direction in the seminary was centered around the ideal of strict obedience. We meditated on the obedience of Jesus and Mary and on the obedience of the apostles and martyrs and saints down through the ages. We were to be like them, spreading the faith by word and deed, remaining always as obedient to those in charge — whether pastor, bishop, or pope — as we would be to Christ himself.

Before ordination all the candidates were required to take the "Oath Against Modernism," though we had only a sketchy idea of what Modernism was all about. The oath had been formulated by Pope Pius X at the beginning of the twentieth century as a barrier against certain liberal theories regarding Scripture and the history of the church circulated by a handful of British and French theologians. We knew little more than their names, since their writings were, of course, in hell. In taking the oath, we "embraced and accepted the unerring teaching authority of the church." We agreed that the faith today had exactly the same meaning as the faith handed down by the apostles, that the church as we know it was "instituted by the historical Christ" and that it "was built upon Peter, the prince of the apostolic hierarchy." We condemned any view suggesting that dogmas may change over time or that Sacred Scripture may be "interpreted in ways contrary to the traditions of the church." In summary, we declared that the "absolute and immutable truth preached by the apostles from the beginning may never be believed to be different, may never be understood in any other way."[2]

Truth be told, I don't think any of us had serious doubts about signing the oath. We had been trained to see the church as the unique beacon of truth. It alone had preserved the message of Christ intact. It alone had full custody of the means of salvation. We knew its members performed daily all over the world the works of mercy, especially among the poor, the disabled, and those denied justice. Yet I believe there was among the men who signed the oath a tinge of queasiness. Like so many other things on the path to the priesthood, the oath was simple, clear, and absolute. No room for exception or hedging: the church was right always, about everything. We were going forth to our assignments as functionaries of that great, changeless institution, as earnest spokesmen for something we didn't fully understand and were forbidden to question. It was all too easy, too cut-and-dried, too hermetically sealed. In the back of my brain I occasionally heard the voice of that grim old man: "We have corrected Thy work."

Unexpected Mutiny

During my years in the priesthood in the middle of the twentieth century, I experienced the church in some of its most noble incarnations — as proclaimer of the good news, as a source of wisdom and counsel, as advocate for peace and justice, as consoler of the dying and grieving. I was even able on occasion to serve in some of these roles. At the same time I came to experience the church in another guise — as sacred hierarchy. The traditional pyramid image of church with the pope at the top and the laity at the bottom had become fixed in the Catholic mind. Everything good and worthy radiated down from above, like manna from heaven, because this was the way Christ had structured his church. "Thou art Peter . . . " was the standard conversation starter and stopper. But was it necessary, I wondered, to make such a spectacle of it?

I had attended ceremonies at the cathedral at which the cardinal archbishop of Chicago processed down the main aisle, resplendent in his crimson and white regalia, behind him at a distance a junior seminarian, whose sole purpose was to hold the cardinal's long, ermine-trimmed train. Ahead had come the knights of Columbus in their medieval costumes and plumed hats, their swords in readiness, and the ranks of monsignors and the lesser priests in cassocks and lacy surplices. Meanwhile, the choir was bursting forth with *"Ecce sacerdos magnus . . . "* ("Behold a great priest who in his days pleased God").

The people in the pews liked all this pomp, it was said, since it was part of a proud, spiritual tradition, just as the Fourth of

July parade was part of our nation's historical tradition. At the same time no one could deny the obvious contradiction between the situation of the church's leadership reveling in its honor and the situation of the same church's founder who had "nowhere to lay his head." But few complained, because this had been the church's public face through most of the second millennium. It was a hierarchy, a class society with clear responsibilities and duties appropriate to the class you belonged to.

Pope Pius X (he of the Oath Against Modernism) put it emphatically in an encyclical, *Vehementer Nos:* The church is "an unequal society" made up of pastors (that is pope, bishops, and clergy) and flock (the laity). In his words: "So distinct are these categories that with the pastoral body only rests the necessary right and authority for promoting the end of the society [that is, the church] and directing all its members toward that end. The only duty of the multitude is to allow themselves to be led, and, like a docile flock, to follow the pastors."

So respectful was the laity toward their priests, these "other Christs," that it was not unknown for a group of Chicago priests eating at a restaurant to discover that their bill had been paid by an anonymous diner at another table. Reverence knew no boundaries. While I was driving to the rectory after playing golf one day, my car stalled in the left-turn lane at an exceptionally busy intersection. To my distress I discovered the car was out of gas, and I was not wearing clerical garb. I sat in stunned helplessness as drivers began to honk in outrage, utter curses, and extend fingers in my direction as they struggled to drive around my vehicle. However, my clerical collar and black coat were in the back seat, so I had the presence of mind to slip quickly into this protective uniform. Instantly the horns and insults ceased. Several drivers pulled over to the side and got out of their cars. "Don't worry, Father," said one. "We'll get you out of this in a jiffy." While two of them directed traffic around me, another got his car behind mine and pushed it gently out of the lane and down the street a half block to a gas station. "Glad to be of help, Father! God bless you, Father," they said. At the time I did not realize this era of uninhibited deference would pass. But as long as it lasted, few priests had problems with the class system. The Catholic community, pastors and flock alike, all had been inculturated into it.

True, the system lent itself to abuse. The arrogance, presumption, or bullying by some priests and bishops was legendary. We called it clericalism, yet it seemed to many a small price to pay for the comfort the church provided: firm rules to live by, grace through the sacraments, a community of fellow believers, eternal salvation. Only a handful rebelled, and these "lost souls" lived in the outer darkness or went over — God help us — to the Protestants.

It is impossible to cite an exact date when everything changed. A shift began in the 1960s when the Second Vatican Council was just beginning. And it gained momentum as the council itself spoke of a new kind of church, no longer at war with the world but sharing in its joys and sorrows. Much of the shift, triggered at that time by the introduction of the birth control pill, was focused on the morality of contraception. Married couples began to talk openly about their frustration with the rhythm method, the lone approved kind of birth control. "The church needs to listen to our experience," they said. "The times have changed."

The official response of leadership to this incipient, entirely unexpected, mutiny was firm and authoritative: "No, nothing has changed. Your so-called experience has no value for moral decision. We the teachers, the magisterium, will tell you what is moral and not moral, as we have always done." Priests like me who were serving in parishes felt as if we were sitting in a stalled automobile with an empty tank.

I could not prevent the words of the Grand Inquisitor from echoing in my head. "They will have no secrets from us. We shall allow or forbid them to live with their wives and mistresses, to have or not to have children . . . and they will submit to us gladly and cheerfully. The most painful secrets of their consciences, all, all they will bring to us and we shall have an answer for all."

The Last Hurrah?

I resigned from the active priesthood in 1970, began a new
career as a journalist, and saw the incipient mutiny become a
prolonged, mostly quiet revolution. Since the magisterium was
unwilling to reconsider birth control or even talk about the other
troubling issues that were emerging (married priests, women's
ordination, remarriage after divorce, homosexuality), Catholics
began to act on their convictions. The revolution was not universal. Many regarded the crisis as a sign of selfishness and
disobedience and continued to function as before like a docile
flock. But something was occurring that seemed almost without
precedent — large numbers of Catholics departing the church,
others declaring themselves permanently inactive, and a great
many, the majority perhaps, staying within the church while vo-
cally disagreeing with church teaching and doctrine, and some
pressing for change. They would not go away and would not
play by the old rules.

It was the sort of expression of freedom that the Grand
Inquisitor had confidently foreseen as doomed to extinction.
Catholics were no longer "marveling" at church leaders, grate-
fully looking on them "as gods" or happily handing over the
freedom which they found so "dreadful." Church leadership —
pope and bishops — had not expected such a sea change. Nor,
as it has turned out, had those pressing for a new kind of open
church expected such sustained resistance from the institution,
such a concerted demand that the wind and waves should cease.
Some forty years after the closing of the Vatican Council little
has changed, except that a whole generation of young Catholics
have given up on the church as an operative agency in their lives.
The level of discouragement on all sides is high.

How will it turn out? Will the Roman Catholic Church become in time a shriveled fossil, influencing only the small number
of the truly faithful? Or will those who have challenged traditional church authority come back, along with their children and
grandchildren, to confess their sins of pride? Or, as some predict,

will the church eventually be restored in numbers and prestige by increasing growth from Africa, Asia, or Latin America, where acceptance of church authority is more in line with the expectations of the Grand Inquisitor? Or will something unforeseen occur? Is God perhaps doing a new thing?

During the 1990s I became fascinated with the church's history and wrote about how it has dealt with some major challenges: new discoveries, shifts in culture, scientific breakthroughs, theological advances. Since history is usually written by the winners, much of the literature I studied emphasized the institutional church as heroic, a long-suffering victor against assaults on its rights and prerogatives by groups ranging from the gnostics of the early days to the modernists and feminists of the twentieth century. The immediate response to almost any new idea or interpretation was negative on the grounds that it went against church tradition. In those cases where a new understanding could not be dismissed, it would be integrated slowly — sometimes over centuries — into the accepted body of authoritative doctrine, as if it had always been there — at least implicitly.

This peculiar dialectic of stolid rejection followed eventually by some kind of resolution is not of course unique to the church. It has been the instinctive style of top-down institutions, whether political dictatorships or major industrial corporations. But through the ages the church has insisted it is essentially different from other earthly institutions. It is the Kingdom of God, a communion of saints and sinners, which will perdure to the end of time because of the ongoing presence of the Holy Spirit promised by Christ. But if the tasks of discernment, decision-making, and governing belong exclusively to the hierarchy, then what we do have is a dictatorship, one sanctioned by the Holy Spirit. And disputes and dissent must be regarded *prima facie* as disobedience to the manifest will of God. If, on the other hand, the presence of the Spirit is an often ambiguous and mysterious presence, moving in unexpected ways and using human instruments as the Spirit chooses, then we would have a less efficient operation and a far more sensitive, participative communion of saints and sinners. The tension between these two interpretations, I believe, is at the heart of much of church history and at the very center of the tensions today.

In the story of the Grand Inquisitor Ivan Karamazov presents the old cardinal as spokesman and embodiment of a rigidly controlling Catholic Church, whose goal is to make humanity obedient and submissive, lest the curse of free will tear the world apart. And he excoriates Jesus for placing so much value on freedom and leaving humanity to its own pitiful devices. So intent is he (and the church he represents) on control, on relieving humanity of "that terrible gift that has brought such suffering" that he rejects the "vague and enigmatic" sayings of Jesus in favor of the practical, take-charge approach of the "wise spirit."

I believe Alyosha is correct in saying Ivan's poem is in defense of Jesus and an ironic condemnation of the excesses of control on the part of the church. The big question remains: Is Ivan correct in this? Has the church misdirected the message of the gospel in favor of naked control? I think history indicates that it has in many situations. And I believe there are intimations of the Grand Inquisitor's approach operative to this day in the policy and polity church. But I would not adopt as true his grim analysis, since I believe in God and the continuing presence of the Holy Spirit's presence in the church. That presence can be observed through the perennial bubbling up from below: in calls for reform, in resentment toward arrogance and arbitrary decisions, in demands to be listened to, to have a voice in what concerns Christian people. It can be heard throughout church history, like a great rumbling underground, though too often dismissed as a manifestation of mischief or drowned out by a chorus of institutional triumphalism.

The purpose of this book is twofold. First, to give witness to that voice in various eras and to state that it represents an essential mark of the Catholic Church. The church is by self-definition one, holy, catholic, and apostolic. I submit it is also by definition meant to be participative, and the neglect of that mark has a lot to do with the chronic animosity that has confronted the church over the centuries. Second, the book argues that the church as consciously participative (even, dare I say, democratic) will come to fruition in this twenty-first century. It may seem foolishly optimistic to make such a prediction when the administration in the Vatican and in most dioceses is far more disposed to defense of the old order than to any consideration of change. But there are many factors present that never were operative before, all pointing to a new kind of church. They cannot be resisted forever. Indeed, fierce resistance to change is often the last hurrah of a faltering regime. Though major change will not come easily or quickly, it will come, and I argue it is the Grand Inquisitor, not Jesus, who will inevitably be sent out into the dark alleys of the town.

Part I

THE PAST

—— ✝ ——

Chapter One

The Community Jesus Founded

———— ✝ ————

You know that among the Gentiles...their rulers lord it over them and their great ones are tyrants.... But it is not so among you. — JESUS TO HIS DISCIPLES, MARK 10:43

WHAT KIND OF LEGACY did Jesus leave behind? What sort of community — if any — did Jesus create to spread his message? How should such a community or church operate, and who should be in charge? These are questions for the ages — still discussed and disputed by scholars. Their writings provide a rich field for study, but it is a field that has been plowed and replowed so often that there's hardly a clod that has not been sliced and diced a thousand times.

As a twelve-year-old student at a Catholic school years ago, I knew nothing of these discussions. The priests and sisters assured us that Jesus founded the Roman Catholic Church, and he meant it to operate exactly as it was operating in our own time: a wise and saintly pope, Pius XII, at the helm, assisted by numberless cardinals, bishops, priests, and sisters. They constituted the hierarchy as far as we sixth graders understood it — and as one particularly grim nun was inclined to settle questions, "Woe betide anyone who thinks otherwise, has doubts about the faith, or forgets to genuflect in church."

Then came the film *The Keys of the Kingdom.* It was a major hit in 1944, starring the young actor Gregory Peck. On the basis of the title, I assumed it would be about the pope and the church and about Jesus delivering the keys of authority to Peter — all ideas we were well schooled in. But when I saw the movie, this was not the case. To be sure, *The Keys of the Kingdom* was about a Catholic priest, but the pope never came up. And the priest, whose life from boyhood to old age was portrayed, was a different kind of person than I expected. As played by Peck, Fr. Francis Chisholm enjoyed little success in his early ministry in Scotland, so his bishop asked him to go to China as a missionary, where he had for much of his career even less success by the church's standards. At one point his cousin, a haughty, condescending bishop (played brilliantly by Vincent Price) informs Chisholm on a visit that his rate of bringing converts to the church is the lowest in an entire region of China. It isn't that Chisholm is lazy or incompetent. The problem is partly his gritty honesty. Early on, it appears, he might have converted an entire city after he helped save the life of the mandarin's son. The mandarin, the respected local leader, is willing to become Catholic out of gratitude, but Chisholm tells him gratitude is not a sufficient reason and politely turns him down. This priest doesn't display his authority or relish his prerogatives. Instead, he lives humbly, extending himself to the people and their needs. He takes in an orphan girl, opens a medical clinic, quietly comforts his dying atheist friend, personally welcomes a newly arrived Protestant missionary to the area, and, in an early version of liberation theology, he assists the local citizenry in repelling an attack by a warlord (for which his church is shelled and left in ruins). Toward the end of his time in China, Chisholm is revered by the people, though his spiritual conquests are meager.

Chisholm's ministry was founded on a deep sense of compassion, a compassion that seems natural and effortless. The film concludes with the priest, old but still active, going fishing with a boy. To my wonderment, as the scene fades these words appear on the screen: "I will give to you the keys to the kingdom of heaven," and below them the citation "Christ to Peter." I was moved by the film and still am on the several times I've seen it since, as I was by the book by author A. J. Cronin on which it was based. I was puzzled as well. Weren't the keys, the symbols of authority, given to Peter and his successors to rule and govern? What does the life of an exceptionally compassionate man have to do with that? Wasn't this a stretch, to title a piece of fiction with a phrase that has an altogether different meaning? Or could it be, I wondered dimly, if this was what the keys were all about in the first place? Only years later did I come to appreciate how closely the movie touched on some major themes of the New Testament.

A System Not of Purity but of Compassion

In the mid-1960s a Scripture scholar named Barnabas Mary Ahern seemed to appear almost out of nowhere. A Passionist priest and seminary professor, he had been a *peritus* (expert) at the Second Vatican Council and was giving talks all over the country about what was for many of us a "new approach" to the Bible. We had been educated to see the biblical books, if not dictated directly by God, at least transmitted so precisely that their meaning, as traditionally explained by the church, was beyond dispute. Wrong, said Fr. Ahern. More than a hundred years of scholarship by Catholic, Protestant, and Jewish experts could not be casually dismissed. Nor, said Ahern and other scholars, like Raymond Brown and John Meier, who attracted wide attention after him, should anyone think that solid historical and literary criticism of the Scriptures is incompatible with faith.

I heard Ahern speak on several occasions, read his articles, and relished his reverently rational approach to the New Testament writings. I became aware that the Gospels are not eyewitness accounts of Jesus' life. Rather, they contain some of Jesus' direct words and actions, but these were adapted and applied to the circumstances of the Christian community as it developed during the last half of the first century. In addition, these writings reflect how belief about who Jesus was also had developed in the community over the years. We were cautioned

not to confuse the Jesus of history with the Christ of faith, since
it is primarily the Christ of faith we meet in the New Testament.
If we accept the ongoing presence of the Holy Spirit in that community, then there is no need to reject such developments. And
so we were alerted to look for the themes that reveal not just
what Jesus said but how it was understood and acted upon by
his earliest followers.

What kind of legacy did Jesus leave and how did he want his
community to operate? The Gospels report such an abundance
of scenes in which Jesus makes clear his abhorrence for the established top-down system of governance in both church and
state that it's impossible, I believe, to think he supported it or
was indifferent to it. Jesus is dogged in reproaching the disciples
whenever they misinterpret his intentions regarding superiority
and inferiority in relationships. He wants them to comprehend
something that is crystal clear to him, and they don't get it. For
the most part, we don't either. A powerful example occurs in the
tenth chapter of the Gospel of Mark when James and John, the
sons of Zebedee, ask to sit, one at Jesus' right hand, the other
at his left, when he passes into glory. It's a bold demand for
the top ruling spots in the coming Kingdom. The other apostles
were livid when they heard about the nerve of the brothers. In
reaction, Jesus called the twelve to him and said,

> You know that among the Gentiles those whom they recog-
> nize as their rulers lord it over them, and their great ones are
> tyrants over them. But it is not so among you; but whoever
> wishes to become great among you must be your servant,
> and whoever wishes to be first among you must be slave of
> all. (Mark 10:43–45)[1]

Whatever form the Kingdom of God will take, indicates Jesus,
its pattern of authority should not resemble that in the governments of this world; in fact, it must operate in a fashion
contradictory to the worldly model.

A similar story occurs in Mark when the apostles had been
arguing about which of them was the greatest.

He sat down, called the twelve, and said to them, "Whoever wants to be first must be last of all and servant of all." Then he took a little child and put it among them; and taking it in his arms, he said to them, "Whoever welcomes one such child in my name welcomes me, and whoever welcomes me welcomes not me but the one who sent me." (Mark 9:35–37)

Again the paradox of first and last is stressed as fundamental. Mark's is believed to be the first written of the four canonical Gospels, around 68 CE when the persecution of Christians was just beginning, and its emphasis reflects some of the problems the community was facing at the time. But variations on the theme, using almost identical words, are found in Matthew's Gospel (20:25–27) written almost twenty years later, around 85, and in Luke's Gospel (9:33–37), written in about 90.

As important as what Jesus said is what Jesus did. Scripture scholars point out the vivid contrast between his approach to the fulfilling of the law and that of the scribes and Pharisees of his time. For him the guiding rule was compassion to those in need. And his entire public life is full of acts of kindness. He feeds the hungry crowd, heals the lepers, cures the blind, casts out unclean spirits, raises up a girl who has died, and saves the life of an adulteress who is about to be stoned. He points out that these acts of service are the signs of the coming kingdom, and at the end, during the Last Supper, Jesus makes sure the apostles understand how all this relates to them.

After he had washed their feet, had put on his robe, and had returned to the table, he said to them, "Do you know what I have done to you? You call me Teacher and Lord — and you are right, for that is what I am. So if I, your Lord and Teacher, have washed your feet, you also ought to wash one another's feet. For I have set you an example, that you also should do as I have done to you. Very truly, I tell you, servants are not greater than their master, nor are messengers greater than the one who sent them. If you know these things, you are blessed if you do them." (John 13:12–17)

In these texts Jesus uses strong language and examples to communicate how his disciples are to operate, among themselves and in their dealings with others. Certainly, it seems, they are to be leaders, but their leadership is not to be authoritarian, autocratic, or despotic. They are to function as servants, and this surely means openness to those they serve, especially since these others are also recipients of the Holy Spirit.

Scholars believe that much of the hostility Jesus aroused was due precisely to his interpretation of what God required of his people. The scribes and Pharisees relied on what has been called a purity system, which carefully distinguished between the just and the unjust, between the pure and the impure. At one extreme were the Jewish religious leaders and other Jews who prided themselves on their scrupulous observance of the law. At the other was a whole caste system of the impure: the chronically ill, especially lepers, the crippled and maimed, women who were menstruating or had just given birth, beggars and the hopelessly poor, those in impure professions such as prostitutes and tax collectors, Greeks, Romans, Samaritans, Gentiles in general, any male who had not been circumcised, and finally those Jews who were unobservant, especially regarding dietary and meal requirements and the proper keeping of the Sabbath.

Although Jesus does not condemn the Mosaic law, he goes out of his way to show his disdain for those who keep the outward aspects of the law but have no regard for its internal meaning. His is a system not of purity but of compassion. And so he eats with the impure, associates with the poor, extends himself and his healing to foreigners and outcasts, breaks the Sabbath laws, and makes a Samaritan the hero in one of his best-known parables. His indignation over empty, external observance drives him to confront the scribes and Pharisees head on:

But woe to you, scribes and Pharisees, hypocrites! For you lock people out of the kingdom of heaven. For you do not go in yourselves, and when others are going in, you stop them. Woe to you, scribes and Pharisees, hypocrites! For you cross sea and land to make a single convert, and you make the new convert twice as much a child of hell as yourselves.... Woe to you, scribes and Pharisees, hypocrites! For you are like whitewashed tombs, which on the outside look beautiful, but inside they are full of the bones of the dead and of all kinds of filth. So you also on the outside look righteous to others, but inside you are full of hypocrisy and lawlessness. (Matt. 23:15–18, 27–28)

What the Gospels give us, I think, is not a full-blown blueprint of how this community of Jesus' followers should function. And in that regard, the Grand Inquisitor was not too far off when he complained that Jesus left us with much that is "exceptional, vague and enigmatic." It is often by negation that we get the message: not a community whose leadership is domineering, not a community whose members are driven by competition to get ahead, not a community that is exclusive or smug, not a community that values outward piety over inward integrity of heart. Rather, it is to be humble, open to all, oriented to service, compassionate. I think that is what the author of *The Keys of the Kingdom* was trying to communicate in the person of Fr. Chisholm and why both the book and film have an enduring fascination.

Of course, there is the more traditional interpretation of those words in Matthew's Gospel, namely, that Jesus is passing on to Peter and his successors supreme juridical authority in the church. "I will give you the keys of the kingdom of heaven, and whatever you bind on earth will be bound in heaven, and whatever you loose on earth will be loosed in heaven" (Matt. 16:18–19). They are words that have been carved in stone on cathedral walls or painted above the high altar of numberless churches. Yet just two chapters later in Matthew, Jesus makes an almost identical pledge, this time to all the disciples: "Truly I tell you, whatever you bind on earth will be bound in heaven, and whatever you loose on earth will be loosed in heaven" (Matt. 18:18). I thought it refreshing — and perhaps more appropriate — when I saw another key saying of Jesus inscribed on the high dome of St. James Cathedral in Seattle, Washington: "I am in your midst as one who serves" (Luke 22:27).

A Community That Makes Decisions

Though the Gospels recount Jesus' life, they are not the earliest Christian writings. For this we have the epistles of St. Paul, which provide a sense of how leadership and members of this spreading compassionate community interacted and reached decisions. Like most young Catholics, I encountered this tireless letter writer almost every Sunday at Mass in the reading before the Gospel. We presumed his works were less important, largely because we sat for his contribution and stood for the Gospel. We knew Peter and Paul as perhaps the most important duo of the early church — the two premier apostles. Only later did I discover that Paul was not an apostle in the traditional sense. He was not one of the twelve whom Jesus chose during his public life. Paul, known as Saul, had been a young Pharisee, zealous in his devotion to the Mosaic law and determined to wipe out the Christian heresy until he was struck by a flash of light one day on his way to Damascus and left temporarily blind. He had a vision of Jesus and discovered he was to become a missionary of Christ to the Gentiles. Paul never looked back, setting out on a three-year journey of evangelization. He eventually met Peter, later the other apostles, in Jerusalem. I can only imagine the suspicion, if not animosity, Paul encountered in those early sessions with the original chosen ones. Somehow he overcame.

We know more about Paul and his travels than we do about all the other apostles put together, and it is generally conceded by scholars that he had more to do with forming the operation of the early church than any other person. Paul did all his travels, wrote all his letters, and was executed in Rome during Nero's persecution, around 63, before even the first of the Gospels was written.

There are seven epistles almost universally regarded as having been authored by Paul himself (1 and 2 Corinthians, 1 Thessalonians, Galatians, Romans, Philemon, and Philippians), all written between 50 and 59. The fact that other works in the New Testament were attributed to him indicates how highly he was regarded by other Christian writers. According to New Testament scholar Stephen Harris, "His ideas and personality so captured the imagination of later Christian writers that they paid tribute to the great apostle by writing in his name and perpetuating his teachings."[2]

What I find noteworthy is that although his letters reveal Paul as an extraordinarily self-confident, Type A personality and organizer, he did not appoint any single person or group as overseer in the churches he founded, nor is there evidence that he gave anyone authority to act in his name. As his writings insist, it was the whole community that constituted the Body of Christ and the bearer of the Holy Spirit. So his teachings, his appeals, his apologies, his scoldings and warnings are invariably sent to the whole community. There are virtually no references to bishops, elders, or other official exercisers of authority. These offices, it seems, had not yet evolved. First Corinthians, for example, is addressed "To the church of God which is at Corinth, to those sanctified in Christ Jesus, called to be saints together with all those who in every place call on the name of our Lord Jesus Christ, both their Lord and ours" (1 Cor. 1:2). First Thessalonians is sent "To the church of the Thessalonians in God the Father and the Lord Jesus Christ: Grace to you and peace: We give thanks to God always for you all, constantly mentioning you in our prayers" (1 Thess. 1:1-2).

This does not suggest a total disregard for leadership on Paul's part. In First Thessalonians, he says, "We beseech you, brethren, to respect those who labor among you and are over you in the Lord and admonish you, and to esteem them very highly in love

because of their work" (1 Thess. 5:12). But Paul was more concerned with the leadership provided by the charisms at work
in the community than with the appointment of persons holding juridical office. In First Corinthians he says, "And God has
appointed in the church first apostles, second prophets, third
teachers; then deeds of power, then gifts of healing, forms of assistance, forms of leadership, various kinds of tongues" (1 Cor.
12:28). It's obvious from the context that Paul was not setting
up some kind of list of superiors and inferiors here; rather, he
was insisting on the basic equality of all parts of the Body of
Christ. And in First Thessalonians he warns against privileging
any of the charisms over the others: "Do not quench the Spirit,
do not despise prophesying, but test everything; hold fast what
is good" (1 Thess. 5:19).

It is the community that makes the decisions. Paul's intent is
not to decree for all time a system of church governance. His
purpose is largely pastoral: to clarify the gospel message, to correct misunderstandings, and to stem the rivalries that apparently
threatened to tear apart these infant communities. "Without im-
posing a dogmatic conformity," says Harris, "[Paul] asks his
readers to work together cooperatively for their mutual benefit."
Christian congregations met in private houses, adds Harris,

> large enough to accommodate the entire group. Although
> membership was limited to perhaps 50 or 100 persons,
> the group was broken into several cliques. Some members
> placed undue importance on the particular leader who had
> converted or baptized them and competed with one another
> over the prestige of their respective mentors. A more seri-
> ous cause of division may have been the members' unequal
> social and educational backgrounds.[3]

In many of these early epistles Paul reaches a profound and
pained eloquence as he begs the faithful to hang together, to
overcome their grudges, to realize that in Christ they are all one:
"For just as the body is one and has many members, and all
the members of the body, though many, are one body, so it is

with Christ" (1 Cor. 12:12). The traditional order of things must
give way, he insists, to something radically new: "There is no
longer Jew or Greek, there is no longer slave or free, there is no
longer male and female; for all of you are one in Christ Jesus"
(Gal. 3:26).

That Paul would extend his idea of gospel equality to women
is both amazing and confusing. In these early writings he men-
tions many women by name and does so in a way that indicates
some held leadership positions in the communities he founded.
In Philippians, chapter 4, he refers to Exodia and Syntyche "who
have worked hard with me to spread the gospel together with
Clement and all my other fellow workers." In Romans, chapter 16, he lists Priscilla (ahead of her husband Aquilla) as "fellow
members in the service of Jesus Christ." Also in Romans 16
he asks the community to assist Phoebe, a leader in another
church, in carrying out her duties. Later in the chapter Paul sends
greetings to some twenty-eight men and women; among them
is Junia, described as "prominent among the apostles." In this
Paul is surely running counter to Greco-Roman culture, which
envisioned women only in the most subordinate roles. Many
scholars contend it is likely that widows and other women who
headed their own houses presided at the Eucharistic meal when
celebrated in their homes.

What is confusing is an unexpected putdown of women,
which appears in First Corinthians: "Women should keep silence
in the churches. For they are not permitted to speak, but should
be subordinate, as even the law says. If there is anything they
desire to know, let them ask their husbands at home" (1 Cor.
14:34–35). Scholars now contend that these two verses, so out
of sync with everything else in his early writings, were not written by Paul; they believe they were inserted long after Paul's
death in an effort to bring Corinthians into harmony with the
anti-woman diatribes in the so-called Pastoral Epistles.

These Pastoral Epistles (First and Second Timothy and Titus)
are among other New Testament writings that were probably
produced in the latter years of the first century or the first part

of the second. They reveal how much the church had been changing since Paul's journeys in the middle of the first century. The fluid, communitarian, participative form of church organization that permeated the communities Paul founded was evolving in some places into a more stratified system with distinct roles and areas of responsibility. These later writings speak often of bishops or overseers, elders or presbyters, and deacons or assistants. In some churches there was emerging what became known as "monarchical bishops" — men whose religious authority was considered supreme and immune to revision or contradiction. What Paul thought of as "churches" had become "the church," a budding institution, self-conscious about preserving itself in unity.

Scripture scholar Raymond Brown notes, "Once the movement associated with Christ became organized enough to be a society called 'church,' it began to decide that certain standards of religious respectability were very important for the common good. Individuals, however talented, who did not meet these standards would have to be sacrificed. The presbyter... had to serve as a model father of a family."[4] The Pastoral Epistles show such a preoccupation with the familial qualities of those called to ministry, notes Brown, that it is unlikely that Paul would have qualified for a leadership post in Titus's church.

The writer of First Timothy wants anyone with new and different ideas to be prevented from teaching: "They must be silenced for they are upsetting whole households by teaching for dishonest profit what they have no right to teach" (1 Tim. 1:3). Says Brown, "In the Pastorals then we have the ancestor of the theology of a deposit of doctrine, and such ecclesiastic developments as the approval of professors, imprimaturs, an index of forbidden books and supervised church presses." The pastorals' rigid approach can be understood in part because the church in the early second century was facing a crisis due to the spread of gnostic doctrines, so the message was not to stray or deviate from the teaching of the apostles. Still, argues Brown, "the great danger of an exclusive stress on officially controlled teaching... is that, having been introduced at moments of crisis, it becomes a consistent way of life."[5]

Equally troubling in the Pastorals is their sexist, if not misogynist, attitude toward women. Second Timothy, for example, typifies women as the members of the community who will inevitably miss the point of sound teaching unless they are given no-nonsense instruction, since false teachers will "make their way into households and captivate silly women, overwhelmed by their sins and swayed by all kinds of desires, who are always being instructed and can never arrive at a knowledge of the truth" (2 Tim. 3:6–7).

Brown is appalled by this effort to corral and control the Holy Spirit. Second Timothy, he says,

> shows no expectation that sometimes women might on their own detect a falsehood peddled to them or might even have something to teach the presbyters. The failure of the author to make allowance for ideas "from the bottom up," as if all perspicacity comes from the top down in the structure, does not prepare the ordinary readers of the Pastorals to play a contributive role in teaching.[6]

Did the church then in less than one hundred years lose completely the participative, open charismatic form it had in the early days? By no means. Many of the later writings stress the community's right to an active role in the church. Especially noteworthy is First Peter's declaration: "But you are a chosen race, a royal priesthood, a holy nation, God's own people" (1 Pet. 2:9). This is hardly a description of passive sheep. Other early books not included in the New Testament also presume an active voice in the full community. The *Didache,* probably written in the early second century, tells Christian churches, "You must then elect for yourselves bishops and deacons who are a credit to the Lord."[7] And "The Apostolic Tradition of St. Hippolytus," perhaps written in the late second or early third century, says, "Let the bishop be ordained, being in all things without fault chosen by all the people. And when he has been proposed and found acceptable to all, the people shall assemble on the Lord's day together with the presbytery and such bishops as may attend."[8] These directives notwithstanding, something was developing that would turn the church as movement into the church as institution during the second and third centuries.

A Church of Many Voices

The one book that treats extensively of decision making in the first years is the Acts of the Apostles. Although probably written about 90, it narrates events, including the coming of the Holy Spirit, the first activities of the apostles and disciples, Paul's conversion and his missionary journeys, all of which occurred thirty or forty years earlier. It therefore reflects themes and emphases present in the primitive Christian community mixed with those of the church as it became more organized and hierarchical. Scholars agree Acts is a very stylized account, with every crisis leading to a successful outcome under the hands-on guidance of the Holy Spirit. Although the leading actors in the book are the two authority figures, Peter and Paul, the Spirit does not work exclusively through them. The Spirit also operates through deacons like Stephen, teachers, elders, prophets, women like Lydia and Priscilla, and ordinary believers.

In a single chapter, Acts 15, the early church is shown facing its first major crisis — one that threatened to tear the community apart permanently. Must Gentiles who accept Christ be obliged also to follow the Mosaic law, including observance of the laws, rituals and eating regulations of the Torah, especially the requirement that all males be circumcised? Or does the New Covenant in Christ supersede the Old Law, so its regulations are no longer required? The apostles were Jews, and many, Peter in particular, initially saw faith in Christ as the next step in Judaism. Jesus, after all, was born a Jew, lived and died as a Jew, and was raised again as a Jew; therefore, provisions of the Law of

Moses remain in effect. Setting them aside could be seen as apostasy. For Paul and many others, however, Christ inaugurated a new creation, the fulfillment and completion of the Mosaic law; therefore, there was no need to press these old obligations on the Gentiles. Convictions and emotions were strong on both sides. On one occasion, Paul reproached Peter to his face on the issue at a public gathering (Gal. 2:11).

It is not known how long the argument raged. But Acts presents a peaceful settlement coming out of one climactic meeting in Jerusalem, perhaps around the year 49. Scholars suggest the writer (identified as Luke but more likely someone writing in his name) may have telescoped many discussions and many meetings over several days, weeks, or months into one event for the sake of emphasis and impact.

Chapter 15 (1–34) describes Paul and Barnabas coming to Jerusalem and being welcomed at a meeting "by the church and the apostles and the elders." Members of the Pharisaic party stood up and insisted the Law of Moses was still a matter of obligation, "So the apostles and elders met together to consider the matter" amid "much debate."

New Testament scholar Luke Timothy Johnson says, "The dynamics of the meeting are not clear. The whole assembly [of believers] appears to be present," although the discussion that follows "seems only to involve the leaders."[9] Then Peter, representing the apostles, rose up, and his words indicated he had changed his mind about requiring Gentile adherence to the Old Law. His reason was the experience he and others had in observing how God gave the Holy Spirit to the Gentiles "just as he did to us." Listening to his narrative, "the whole assembly kept silence." Next, they listened as Paul and Barnabas, representing the missionary outreach, told of the "signs and wonders" they had seen God working among the Gentiles. Finally, James, called the brother of Jesus and the leader of the Jerusalem community, stepped forward. It might have been expected that he would be outspoken in disagreeing with the previous speakers and in defending the continued legality of the Old Law. He did not; instead, he agreed with them, citing the Prophet Amos's vision of God making his name known to all the nations. "Therefore," said James, "I have reached the decision that we should not trouble those Gentiles who are turning to God." As an apparent concession to Jewish law, he recommended that the Gentile converts be required to maintain at least a few token Jewish restrictions.

The resolution, according to Acts, was agreed on by the "apostles and elders, with the consent of the whole church," and a letter was drafted, explaining the decision. Paul and Barnabas, along with two other leaders, were delegated to travel to the Gentile communities with the news. When they arrived, the new churches heard the message that "it has seemed good to the Holy Spirit and to us to impose on you no further burden than these essentials." All were greatly relieved, and, says Acts, "rejoiced at the exhortation." When the messengers left, "they were sent off in peace by the believers to those who had sent them."

At first glance, chapter 15 could be seen as an example of the hierarchical church in action; the top leadership discusses the issue, finally comes to a conclusion, and the faithful obey. But Johnson is among scholars who see a lot more going on. It is true James makes the judgment, says Johnson, but he "does not decide alone. The apostles and elders must agree *with the whole Church* for that decision to be carried. In fact, it is not enough for the Mother Church to decide the issue unanimously."[10] The local churches must also express their agreement and "send the emissaries back 'in peace' for the decision truly to have been reached." In Johnson's judgment, there is participation by the community, though we do not know the extent of their involvement in the debate — other than the Pharisees rising up to argue their case.

Furthermore, says Johnson, Acts 15 has "a paradigmatic character" because it

enables the reader to see the early Church reaching decision
by means of an articulation of faith, as a process of discernment of God's activity. Priority is given to the narratives of
faith, for it is such narratives which enable private religious experience to reach the level of public discernment.
Here Peter does not appear as the judge but as another
witness.... Here Paul and Barnabas do not appear as advocates pleading a case but as simple witnesses of "the signs
and wonders God has done . . . among the Gentiles."[11]

This meeting, sometimes called the Council of Jerusalem, thus
typifies, in Johnson's view, how the church should make decisions for all time: by listening to many voices, by discerning
where the Spirit, who is always out ahead of the church, is
leading:

We must let go of any fantasy concerning the church as
a stable, predictable, well-regulated organization. If the
church is truly the place in the world where the experience
of God is brought to the level of narrative and discernment, then the church will always be disorderly, a family
living under stress, because it will be a community always
in transition between partial closure and openness.[12]

Johnson suggests that a commitment to discernment, as ex-
emplified in the Acts of the Apostles, could mightily assist the
church in reaching closure on some of its thorniest controversies.
As one example, he asks,

How can the church today know whether it should reverse
two thousand years of precedent and ordain women? It
cannot know unless it undertakes to discern the activity
of God in the women of the church today, which can be
made available only by the narrative of that activity by the
faithful. Such a commitment to discernment requires . . . the
conviction that God is active in the lives of all, including the lives of women. The symbolisms of the past will
remain intact, and indeed petrified, without the stimulus

provided by the work of the Holy Spirit. The Scripture will be heard to say the same thing over and over again eternally, unless our hearing is renewed by the story inscribed among us even now by the finger of God. Without the narrative of the experience of God, discernment cannot begin. And without such discernment, I would argue, decisions are theologically counterfeit.[13]

What kind of church did Jesus intend? No one-size-fits-all answer is possible, but I believe there are potent hints from the earliest days that point to a church of many voices, of openness to ongoing change, and of sensitivity to the Spirit that moves in unexpected ways. And I suspect that many Catholics are beginning to see that as the direction in which the church must go.

Chapter Two

A Man for All Seasons

———— ✝ ————

It has been a resolve of mine right from the beginning . . . to do nothing on my own private judgment without your counsel and the consent of the people.

— CYPRIAN OF CARTHAGE

T HERE ARE SOME Catholics today who still think the Catholic Church is "the true church" because it has never changed. Other religions and other Christian denominations churn and turn, evolve and revolve over the ages, but not Catholicism; it is exactly now what it's been from the beginning, only bigger and better. That idea has been repeatedly refuted by scholars, and its persistence among apologists over the years is rivaled only by the flat-earth theory espoused by a core of true believers. Theologian and historian Francine Cardman says "Catholic literalism" — the assumption that the way things are now is the way they must have been then — is "like looking through the wrong end of a telescope. From this myopic viewpoint, we can only see ourselves. It's no wonder then that we often equate tradition with 'what we've always believed, taught and done.'"[1]

Though much of the historical record is more opaque than transparent, it's clear that the concepts of clergy and laity were absent in the early church and that they came about gradually, as did certain beliefs, rites, and convictions about what was central to the community. Cardman speaks about the church of the second century CE as a loosely connected network "with no centralized authority or authorities, no uniform structures of ministry, no formally recognized canon of Christian Scripture, no official commissions to approve or write liturgical texts, no mechanisms for decision making beyond local communities. Yet over the course of that century, an informal, rough consensus began to emerge in Eastern and Western churches in regard to basic beliefs and practices, as well as to some ecclesial structures necessary to sustain these developments." For example, the "proper procedures" for administering baptism were circulated in a document called the *Didache* and adopted by many communities. "We do not know who the author/compiler of the *Didache* was, nor why he took on the task of producing this document," says Cardman, "nor what authority he hoped it would carry.... What we can surmise, nevertheless, is that liturgical rites came to be accepted through the very act of using them. That is to say, they arose from practice and were recognized as received in practice. In the first and early second centuries then, it was laypeople who created, used and adopted these rites."

Slowly, the roles of bishop, presbyter, and deacon grew more important, and distinctions were drawn between these official, clerical leaders and the masses of the laity. Irenaeus, an extraordinarily influential bishop of the second century, stressed the importance of "apostolicity," that is, a connection between the original twelve and the bishops who were beginning to head each of the scattered Christian communities. Notes Cardman, "Emphasis started to shift from the entire church (all believers) as preserving and passing on the faith, to the bishops as the especially designated successors of the apostles and the teachers of the apostolic faith." By the middle of the third century, the transition was nearly complete, though disputed at times by gnostics and other groups.

A Different Time and Place

I wondered if it might be possible to look intensely at that midpoint to determine how like or unlike church authority was then,

as compared to today. I also wondered if an examination of that
period could discern aspects of church authority that are essential for all time. One of the most likely sources of information
was Cyprian, the bishop of Carthage in North Africa from 248
to 258. At the time Carthage was one of the four great cities of
the Roman Empire, along with Antioch, Alexandria, and Rome.
Located near the present city of Tunis, it had an exceptionally
large Christian population, and, in Cyprian, it had one of the
most prolific and self-assured bishops of all time. Through his
words, I hoped to view Catholicism as it was being lived some
1,750 years ago.

After gathering his writings from several libraries, I was struck
first of all by the great chasm between his time and ours. This
was the age of the martyrs when Christians faced sporadic periods of persecution, ranging from fines and exile to torture and
death. Tradition says Cyprian had been a single, wealthy land-
holder, a rhetorician, and a prominent citizen before converting
to Christianity, probably in his mid-forties. Within four years
he had become the bishop of Carthage, just one year before the
announcement of another crackdown. The church had been left
in peace for some thirty-eight years, but the Roman Empire was
celebrating the beginning of its second millennium. And the emperor, Decius, deemed it appropriate and necessary that citizens
demonstrate their piety and patriotism by making public sacrifice to the Roman gods. Those who refused were considered
disloyal to both church and state and subject to the charge of
treason. Only Jews were exempt from the requirement to sacrifice, largely because they kept to themselves and did not attempt
to make converts. Christians, on the other hand, were a tirelessly
missionary lot, their numbers were growing rapidly, and they
thus seemed a threat to good order. The government saw them
as atheists, since they denied the very existence of the Roman
deities.

Christians had five choices: openly refuse the order and face
the consequences; carry on their lives as usual and hope they
would be overlooked by the authorities; go into hiding; obtain

by bribery or forgery a certificate testifying that they had offered sacrifice when, in fact, they had not; or comply with the requirement as demanded. The latter two choices were expressly forbidden by the church; those who obtained a false certificate or offered sacrifice were considered guilty of apostasy. The concept of mental reservation was not operative in the church at this time. No one was allowed to excuse his real or apparent cooperation with the order to sacrifice on the grounds that he acted due to extreme pain or the threat of death. Such distinctions, in general use in modern times, were of no avail in those dread days.

I found it difficult to imagine the sheer panic that would surely have invaded the Christian community. A great number of Christians reportedly complied with the emperor's decree, but many did not. The most likely believers to be personally summoned or hunted down were the church leaders, so Cyprian chose to go into hiding outside the city, communicating with his people and running the church by a stream of letters and lengthy treatises on subjects like patience and mortality. If there was panic in the Christian community, it was not apparent in Bishop Cyprian, though he knew his whereabouts could be discovered at any time. (He survived the Decian persecution but would be martyred some seven years later under Emperor Valerian.)

As he confronts the persecution of Decius, there is an almost preternatural sense of peace and calm and orderliness about him, as if imprisonment, torture, and death were quite normal and expected experiences — the one sure sign that the faithful are on the right path to an eternal crown. He shows not the slightest anger or bitterness toward the emperor or his Roman enforcers.

"Now, were it possible for us to escape from death, then dying would sensibly be something we might fear," he writes to the laity. "But as man, being mortal, has no option not to die, then let us grasp the opportunity that now comes thanks to God's promise and providence; let us bring our lives to an end,

winning at the same time the reward of immortality."[2] In a letter
to the imprisoned and the condemned, he says, "No blandish-
ments should seduce the unsullied steadfastness of our faith, nor
threats terrify, no tortures and torments overwhelm, for greater
is He who is within us than he who is in the world: the divine
protection has greater power to raise us up than earthly anguish
can avail to cast us down."[3]

You get a sense of a long tradition of terrible suffering and un-
timely death etched into this community, though the prevailing
emotion is not grief but a kind of fatalistic jubilation. In another
letter he announces that he has admitted a man named Celerinus to the level of clergy after he had been finally released from
prison. "For a period of nineteen days he was shut up... under
close guard, in chains and iron," Cyprian writes. "But though
his body was in bondage, his spirit remained unfettered and free.
His flesh grew emaciated by prolonged hunger and thirst, but his
soul, living by faith and courage, God nourished with spiritual
sustenance.... Fettered his feet may have been but the serpent
was downtrodden, crushed and conquered." Cyprian adds that
Celerinus comes from good stock, noting that his grandmother,
Celerina, "long ago received a martyr's crown" and his uncles
Laurentinus and Egnatius, "by their illustrious sufferings merited
palms and crowns from the Lord."[4]

Meanwhile, Cyprian insists that the daily care of the poor go
on as if life were normal. His letters make clear that he has a
sizable population of clerics, including presbyters (or priests),
deacons, subdeacons, acolytes, exorcists, and lectors. In a letter
to them, he says, "The poor... must be cared for to the extent
possible, provided, that is, they remain standing with faith un-
shaken and have not forsaken the flock of Christ. You should
take earnest care that they are provided with the means for allevi-
ating their poverty."[5] In another letter he announces he is sending
"in cash one hundred thousand sesterces, which have been collected from the contributions of the clergy and laity.... This is for
you to distribute with your wonted diligence" to the poor and to

families torn apart by the persecution.[6] According to commentators, that amount would be enough to sustain twelve thousand for a month.

The gentle Cyprian disappears at times, especially when the subject is clerics who are giving communion to lapsed Christians who have not done penance or who are offering sacrifice to the Roman gods as proxies for Christians in prison (an innovation church leaders did not approve of). "What peril indeed have we not reason to fear when the Lord is so offended, seeing that some presbyters . . . are doing something that was totally unknown under our predecessors — with insult and scorn for their bishop they arrogate entire authority to themselves."[7]

And his concern rises to the level of rage whenever he learns the latest activities of the schismatic Bishop Novatian and his allies who have been trying to stir up trouble for Cyprian in Rome. In a letter to Cornelius, the pope, he writes, "Look how high and mighty they make themselves! Look at the puffed-up and bladder-mouthed boasting that goes into their empty menaces — there in Rome, they threaten me behind my back, whereas it is in their power to confront me face to face in Carthage."[8]

An Overwhelming Vote of the People

Observing the several sides of Cyprian, I see an attentive, often pastoral leader who is very conscious of his position and prerogatives and who does not suffer fools (or enemies) gladly. The translator of Cyprian's letters, G. W. Clarke, says, "It is easy to give undue and therefore misleading emphasis to the authoritarian, if not autocratic, interpretation which Cyprian placed on his duties toward his subjects."[9] To do so, it seems to me, would miss the one characteristic that so totally separates the operation of his episcopacy from what we have come to take for granted in modern times. Over and over, in his correspondence, he emphasizes that the full church, especially the laity, are to have a voice and a choice in the major decisions of his diocese, Furthermore, he assumes that this practice is not unique to him or a mere personal preference; it is, he says, the way the church is supposed to operate everywhere. Some examples:

• While the persecution of Decius was still under way, Cyprian became concerned that some of his priests were routinely absolving members of the church who had offered sacrifices to the Roman gods. They were doing this on the recommendation of certain confessors (those who had suffered imprisonment and torture) and letters from the martyrs (those who had made recommendations in prison before they were executed). Cyprian says the practice of quick and easy absolution must be stopped until the persecution had ceased, at which time he will call a diocesan council and a uniform policy of reconciliation will be approved. Writing to his clergy, many of whom wanted quick answers, he says, "I can make no reply on my own, for it has been a resolve of mine, right from the beginning of my episcopate, to do nothing on my own private judgment without your counsel *and the consent of the people*. But as soon as by God's favour I have come to you, we will then discuss in council together."[10]

That this declaration was not just a slip of the tongue is fortified by another letter addressed expressly to the laity: "When, through God's mercy, we have come to you and the bishops have been called together, a large number of us will be able to examine the letter of the blessed martyrs and their requests, acting in conformity with the discipline of the Lord and in the presence of the confessors, *and in accordance also with your judgment*."[11]

Cyprian, whose moral authority extended well beyond the boundaries of the Carthage diocese, summoned several regional councils during his decade as bishop. Though records of their deliberations have not survived, it seems probable that he would have insisted that these gatherings also involve participation by all levels of the church, not just the bishops.

• While in hiding, Cyprian could not confer with his clergy or gather the community together, yet he felt compelled to enroll several confessors who had undergone severe hardships into the

ranks of the clergy. They included the above-mentioned Celerinus and two others. In three letters to the church, the first of
which is addressed "to the Presbyters, deacons and all the laity,"
he is almost apologetic in explaining why he acted without their
involvement. "Dearest brothers," he says, "it is our custom when
we make appointments to clerical office to consult you before-
hand, and in council together with you to weigh the character
and qualities of each candidate."[12] In these cases, he adds, that
was not possible, but he feels certain that the bravery and fi-
delity of these witnesses is such that "they surely already have
the Lord's approbation."

• More compelling evidence of his habitual regard for consultation can be observed in Cyprian's statements about the
selection of bishops in the church. When critics questioned the
legitimacy of the selection of a certain Spanish bishop, Sabinus,
Cyprian rushes in to defend the process that had been followed:
"We can see that divine authority is . . . the source of the practice
whereby bishops are chosen in the presence of the laity," he declares, "and they are judged as being suitable and worthy after
scrutiny and testimony." For confirmation of his statement, he
cites the Old Testament book of Numbers, in which Eleazar is
made a priest in the presence of the assembled people.

God directs that his priest is to be invested before all the
assembled people; that is to say, He is instructing and
demonstrating to us that priestly appointments are not to
be made without the cognizance and attendance of the
people, so that in the presence of the laity any iniquities
of the wicked can be revealed and the merits of the good
proclaimed, and thus an appointment may become right *if
it has been examined and judged, and voted on by all.*[13]

This rule appears also in the New Testament, Cyprian says,
when it was necessary to find a replacement for Judas:

Now the whole congregation was called together and great
caution and scrupulousness was here being exercised just so

as to avoid that anyone unworthy might sidle his way into the service of the altar or the dignity of bishop.... Hence we should show sedulous care in preserving a practice which is *based on divine teaching and apostolic observance,* a practice which is indeed faithfully followed among us and in practically every province. And it is this: when an episcopal appointment is to be duly solemnized, all the neighboring bishops in the same province convene for the purpose along with the people for whom the leader is to be appointed; the bishop is then selected in the presence of the people, for they are the ones who are acquainted most intimately with the way each has lived his life, and they have had the opportunity thoroughly to observe his conduct and behavior.

This exact procedure was adhered to in the consecration of Sabinus, he adds, "following *the verdict of the whole congregation* and in conformity with the judgment of the bishops."[14]

Theologian Francis Sullivan notes that Cyprian repeatedly uses the Latin word *suffragio* (from which the English word "suffrage" is derived) to denote how the whole congregation made its will known. It may be rendered as "verdict," or, more accurately, as "vote." We do not know how the vote or verdict was arrived at in selection of bishops, whether by vocal acclamation, applause, show of hands, or some other means. Vote by ballot was probably impractical, though not inconceivable.

I think it is fascinating that the church in the year 250 had such high regard for the voice of the faithful in selecting leaders. If that practice, based on "divine teaching and apostolic observance," had not been abandoned and had survived into our own day, it seems to me highly probable that many of the church's leadership crises of this early twenty-first century would have been averted.

• Unfortunately, we do not have transcripts of any meetings Cyprian presided over, but we do have correspondence between him and Cornelius, the pope. It gives a brief glimpse of the participative role the laity played in determining who should and who should not be reconciled to the church when the Decian persecution at last ceased. If those who offered sacrifice or obtained forged certificates showed true sorrow for their apostasy, they were to do penance for certain periods of time (or indefinitely) before being absolved of their sin. However, the whole church was involved in deciding who was truly repentant. Describing a great gathering of his church, he writes to Cornelius:

> Oh how I wish, dearly beloved brother, that you could be present here with us when those who make their way back from schism are warped and twisted sinners! Then you would see under what difficulties I labor to persuade the brethren [the whole congregation] to show forbearance, to stifle their feelings of bitter resentment, and to consent that these evildoers should be let in and given healing treatment. They do indeed show delight when those who come back are good enough people whose sins are less offensive; but correspondingly, they put up noisy protests and resistance whenever those who would return to the Church are diehard and shameless sinners, contaminated with adulteries and pagan sacrifices, and yet, to crown it all, still remaining arrogant. . . . It is with enormous difficulty that I manage to persuade my people [a word he consistently uses referring to the laity]. I really extort it out of them — that they allow the admission of such sinners.[15]

In fact, he adds, the resentment expressed by people during this process has proven reasonable because, in some cases, those received back "through my leniency" turned out to be incapable of serving their penance.

Why doesn't Cyprian, the sole bishop of Carthage and Christian leader of the entire region, decide, perhaps with some advice from his inner circle of clergy, who is worthy and who not? Why does he feel it necessary to subject himself and the rest of the church to what had to have been a tumultuous and rowdy experience? Why, as he admits, does he have to plead and beg his people to accept back the sinners, especially when he's forced to acknowledge that in some instances the people knew better than he who deserved reconciliation? Such a lowering of himself would be considered shamefully inappropriate and beneath the dignity of the episcopacy today. Cyprian does not explain. He did it, I think, for the same reason he insisted the vote of the people was necessary in the selection of bishops; it was, in short, a matter of "divine teaching and apostolic observance."

And we have the letter Cornelius wrote back to Cyprian, saying, in effect, the procedure is the same in Rome. He describes a gathering of bishops and presbyters to consider what should be done about a number of lapsed Christians who hope to be reconciled. "Naturally," he says, "the faithful [that is, the laity] had to be notified of all these proceedings so they might see installed in their church the very people whom they had seen...wandering and straying away from it for so long. When their feelings on the matter had been ascertained, a great number of our congregation assembled together. With one voice they all gave thanks to God, expressing in tears the joy in their hearts." These penitents were then absolved, says Cornelius, "amid wildly enthusiastic acclamation from the people."[16] This last phrase uses the word *suffragio* in the original Latin, as Francis Sullivan noted in regard to the appointment of bishops, and therefore might be more accurately translated "with an overwhelming *vote* of the people."[17]

It is not by accident that so much of Cyprian's written legacy has been preserved. He was recognized in his time as an outstanding example of what a bishop should be, and his statement about resolving "to do nothing on my own private judgment without your counsel and the consent of the people" has become one of the most frequently cited sayings in Christian history. It is echoed in the well-known declarations of other early churchmen. Pope Celestine I put it this way in the fourth century, "A bishop should not be given to those who are unwilling to receive him." And Pope Leo I in the next century stated, "Let the one who is going to govern over all be elected by all."[18]

I think these aphorisms reflect Christians' instinctive recognition that full participation by the whole body reflects the radical equality of the apostolic era; the tongues of fire came on everyone in the upper room at Pentecost. Many years after that era, the fire was still aglow in Carthage and warmed other notable centers of Christianity as well. But in the centuries that followed, participation would come to be recognized more and more in the breach than in its observance. By the second millennium it would virtually cease to be recognized as an essential ingredient of the lived faith — except at various times and in certain places where the embers flared up again. Obviously then, the church changes over time, sometimes for the better, sometimes not.

Chapter Three

A Rising Up of the Faithful

———— ✝ ————

The divine tradition committed to the infallible church was proclaimed and maintained far more by the faithful than by the Episcopate. — JOHN HENRY NEWMAN

T HE FOURTH CENTURY witnessed one of the strongest and most sustained examples of the voice of the faithful in the whole course of church history. In 313 the Emperor Constantine granted toleration to all religions with special preference for Christianity. So instead of fearing when the next imperial persecution might begin, Christians found themselves respected, even honored citizens. New churches were erected, bishops were publicly consecrated, priests and deacons were ordained in unprecedented numbers. Catechumens seeking to be baptized appeared everywhere. For the first time since Jesus, Christians had the leisure to think in a detailed way about the content of their faith. Not surprisingly, one of the first questions was, who was Jesus?

> A great prophet, yes.
> The anointed of God, yes.
> The savior of the world, yes.
> The Word (Logos) of the Father, yes.

On these issues, there was general agreement in the church. But who was Jesus in himself? Two conflicting theories began to emerge. One said Jesus might be rightly regarded as the Son of God and the Word of the Father in a metaphorical sense, but he could not be called equal to God. Rather, he was the Father's

supreme and ultimate creation, superior in his inner substance
or nature to any other creature. The Greek expression for this
was *homoiousios* (*homoi* meaning "similar" and *ousios* meaning "substance"). Jesus was said to be of a substance "similar"
to that of God. The priest Arius of Alexandria was the principal
proponent of this position, and it had a strong appeal to intellectuals, especially in the East, since it seemed to preserve the
unique, transcendent nature of God.

The other theory maintained Jesus, the Word of God, was
really and truly God, not metaphorically but literally. He could
be called God and worshipped as fully equal to the Father in
his divinity and eternity. The operative word for this position
was *homoousios* (*homo* meaning "same" and *ousios* meaning
"substance"). The absence of that one Greek letter, *iota,* totally changed the meaning (and thereby gave birth to the popular
saying about two objects not having "an iota of difference"). Advocates of the *homoousios* position included many bishops and
great numbers of the laity who had for generations been speaking
and praying to Jesus as equal to the Father in prayers and liturgies.

The debate was becoming so acrimonious that Constantine
feared it might permanently split the church on a fundamental
teaching. He summoned all the bishops of both the East and
West to meet in a council at Nicaea, a city in present-day Turkey.
Some three hundred bishops attended, most from the Eastern
churches, their expenses paid for by the emperor. The pope was
not present, although he sent a representative; there was no lay
representation. Amid much discussion and no little confusion,
the council published a creed, which said Jesus, the Word, the
Son of God, was "consubstantial" with the Father, that is, of the
same substance (*homoousios*) as the Father, and was therefore
eternal and uncreated. To make this very clear the creed spoke
of the Word as "God from God, light from light, true God from
true God, begotten, not made, one in being with the Father. ... "
A slightly amended version of this original Nicene Creed is still
recited weekly in Catholic liturgies and in the liturgies of some
other Christian denominations.

A Council Rejected by the Bishops

When I studied church history in the seminary, we joked about *homoousios* and *homoiousios*. We were satisfied that Nicaea had settled the old dispute once and for all and that the Arians had packed their bags and quickly faded away. About thirty years later I found out they didn't. While scanning the shelves of a library looking for a certain book, I spotted a small volume, almost a pamphlet, titled *On Consulting the Faithful in Matters of Doctrine.* The title grabbed my attention and I had read most of the book before I checked it out of the library. The author, John Henry Newman, I recognized as a convert to Catholicism from Anglicanism and perhaps the most influential theologian of the nineteenth century. As students we heard about his conversion, his loyalty to the church, and his great books like *Apologia pro Vita Sua* and *A Grammar of Assent.* But we never studied anything he wrote. In this book I encountered Newman's exhaustive study of the history of Nicaea and gained new ideas about the laity's proper role within the church.

After the council the Arians, who followed the teachings of Arius, did not disappear. They put on a major campaign to overturn the decision of the council. During the next fifty-six years they very nearly succeeded in making the whole church Arian. In this they were encouraged by Constantine, who seemed to be leaning toward the Arian view in his latter days, and by his son, Constantius, who succeeded his father as emperor and proved aggressively supportive of that view.

An endless succession of synods and councils over the years served mainly to exacerbate the problem, Newman shows. An outspoken opponent of the Arian position, Athanasius, bishop of Alexandria, was accused of rebellion, sedition, tyranny, murder, sacrilege, and magic during synods of bishops meeting at Caesarea and Tyre in 335. He was deposed, banished to Gaul, and forbidden to ever set foot again in Alexandria. However, six years later, a council in Rome, with 50 bishops present, pronounced Athanasius innocent and obtained his reinstatement.

It was of short duration; later that same year some 90 bishops at Antioch vetoed the decision in Rome, installed an Arian as bishop of Alexandria, and produced four alternate creeds denying that the Word is consubstantial with the Father.[1]

In 347 a council at Sardica, with 350 bishops present, broke up before it even got started over the question of whether or not Athanasius should even be permitted to attend. The pro-Athanasian cohort met separately, excommunicated the pope for allegedly supporting the Arians, and attempted to restore Athanasius and other exiled bishops to their dioceses. Meanwhile, the Arian coalition began to come apart at a council in Sirmium, breaking into two contentious divisions, pure Arians and semi-Arians. With no solution in sight, many dioceses in both the East and West found themselves with two, sometimes, three bishops calling each other heretics and each representing a different position on *homoousios* and consubstantiality.

At a council in Milan in 355, nearly 300 of the bishops in attendance rallied to the Arian cause. And two years later Pope Liberius, under pressure from Emperor Constantius, signed a statement confirming the banishment of Athanasius, thus placing the papacy in the Arian camp. Many more bishops who had at first been steadfast in supporting Nicaea lost hope. At a council at Salucia in 359 only a dozen of the 150 bishops there backed the Nicene position, and at a council in Armenium almost 400 bishops sided with the Arians.

Furthering the momentum, Constantius began to authorize intimidation, persecution, and even military force to bring holdouts to their knees. Jerome, the translator of the Bible into Latin, looked at the situation in 363 and reported, "Nearly all the churches of the whole world under the pretence of peace and the emperor, are polluted with the communion of the Arians.... The Catholics of Christendom were surprised indeed that [their rulers] had made Arians of them."

Meanwhile, Athanasius, never budging from his position, railed against the doctrines of Arius.[2] A popular saying of the time was "Athanasius against the world." And a small group of like-minded clerics, including Basil the Great, Hilary of Poitiers, and Gregory Nazianzen, also remained adamant in their position. Wrote Hilary in frustration, "While we fight about words, inquire about novelties, take advantage of ambiguities...and prepare to anathematize each other, there is scarce a man who belongs to Christ." And late in the conflict Gregory said, "If I must speak the truth, I feel disposed to shun every conference of Bishops; for never I saw one synod brought to a happy issue...and not rather aggravating existing evils."

The Rebellion of the Laity

So why aren't we all Arians? Why didn't the campaign succeed, and how did the creed of Nicaea survive the onslaught? It was the laity, says Newman in *Consulting the Faithful*. Though virtually the entire hierarchy yielded to what seemed inevitable, the vast majority of the lay Catholic world would not — and many paid for their determination. Newman provides more than two dozen reports from those hectic times.[3]

In Constantinople those who insisted on holding the doctrine of consubstantiality were expelled from the churches and many were exiled from the city. Others were forced to receive communion from Arian priests, tortured, or had their property confiscated. In Edessa a Roman prefect was ordered to slay Nicene supporters who had gathered at a major church. When he arrived with his military force, he found that the citizens, instead of fleeing, were hurrying to enter the church and inquired of one woman who had a small child with her, "Have you not heard that the prefect is about to put to death all that shall be found there?" "Yes," replied the woman, "and therefore I hasten, that I may be found there." He asked, "And whither are you dragging that little child?" She responded, "That he also may be vouchsafed the honour of martyrdom." Believing that the whole crowd was prepared to die, the prefect called off the soldiers. While this story and others like it strain credibility, they reflect the general attitude of absolute intransigence that characterized the era.

In Samasota when an Arian bishop was installed, "none of the inhabitants of the city, whether poor or rich, servants or mechanics, husbandmen or gardeners, men or women, young or old" would have anything to do with him. When he entered the public baths, everyone else reportedly stayed out, and even after he left, the people refused to enter the baths because they believed "the water had been contaminated by his heresy." Even in Rome Pope Liberius, who had signed an Arian document, "found the mind of the mass of men alienated from him because he had so shamefully yielded to Constantius." On occasion, the alienation went to extremes. It was reported that George, the Arian bishop installed after Athanasius's removal, was lynched by a pagan mob.

In Syria, Cappadocia, Nicomedia, Armenia, and throughout Egypt and other centers of Christianity, pressure on the people proved largely ineffective, according to the accounts of the day. I found myself asking, why would ordinary Christian laypersons, many illiterate and theologically untrained, remain so strong on a matter of interpretation, and a subtle one at that? In part, the answer may be that subtleties of interpretation were of greater interest to these fourth-century citizens than we imagine, that they believed their religion was not merely the preserve of the hierarchy. Gregory of Nyssa wrote a stimulating, and somewhat tongue-in-cheek account about how the controversy had become a matter of common interest and intense discussion in Constantinople: "The whole city is full of it, the squares, the market places, the cross-roads, the alleyways, the old-clothes men, money changers, food sellers: they are all busy arguing. If you ask someone to give you change, he philosophizes about the Begotten and the Unbegotten; if you inquire about the price of a loaf, you are told by way of reply that the Father is greater and the Son inferior; if you ask, 'Is my bath ready,' the attendant answers that the Son was made out of nothing."[4]

In the late 370s the Arian campaign lost momentum, and at the Council of Constantinople in 381, the creed of Nicaea (in slightly altered form), incorporating its concepts of *homoousios* and consubstantiality, was surprisingly affirmed by 150 bishops from the Eastern branch of Christianity — where the Arian idea had begun and where it originally had its strongest support. It would appear that at long last enough bishops of influence were finally paying attention to the testimony of the people. Unfortunately, most of the proceedings of the council have been lost. However, the Council of Constantinople has come to be regarded in Catholic history as definitive on the subject of Jesus' divinity; it is the church's second, official ecumenical council, the first being the one at Nicaea.

At the time Newman wrote this account, he was under fire from his own bishop in Birmingham, England, and from conservative Catholics for his suggestion in a magazine article that the bishops of England would be well advised "to know the sentiments of an influential portion of the laity before taking any step which they could not recall."[5] It may seem an innocent enough comment to us, but at the time it was viewed as an assault on the sovereign rights of the hierarchy. Newman was informed he was to be removed from his position as editor of *The Rambler* magazine, and *On Consulting the Faithful in Matters of Doctrine* was, in fact, his response; it became the entire contents of the last *Rambler* issue he edited. It's worth noting, I think, that countless histories of the Catholic Church cite the decisions at Nicaea and Constantinople without even mentioning those fifty-six years of turmoil between the two councils. They were likely seen as just one of those glitches in the otherwise smooth unfolding of Catholicism over two millennia. Newman saw those years from a different perspective: as exemplifying a profound truth about the church — a truth that church leadership did not want to acknowledge during most of the fourth century and that it has been loath to acknowledge ever since.

The People Prevail

A terrible mistake is made, contends Newman, when decisions regarding teaching, even dogmas, are made without consulting the sense of the faithful (*sensus fidelium*) or the agreement of the faithful (*consensus fidelium*). Such consultation, he argues, should not be seen as a mere act of kindness or courtesy toward the laity; rather it is an absolute necessity, one of the essential ways the church comes to know its tradition. In the Arian crisis, the many intervening synods and councils between Nicaea and Constantinople spun their wheels, ignoring this important input from below. And the leadership finally righted itself when it realized the voice of the faithful could not be muffled. Newman is exceptionally strong in making his point:

> The Nicene dogma was maintained during the greater part of the fourth century...not by the unswerving firmness of the Holy See, Councils, or Bishops, but...by the *consensus fidelium*. On the other hand, then, I say, that there was a temporary suspense of the *Ecclesia docens* [the teaching church]. The body of the Bishops failed in their confession of the faith. They spoke variously, one against another; there was nothing after Nicaea, of firm, unvarying, consistent testimony, for nearly sixty years. There were untrustworthy Councils, unfaithful Bishops; there was weakness, fear of consequences, misguidance, delusion, hallucination, endless, hopeless, extending itself into nearly every corner of the Catholic Church. The comparatively few who remained faithful were discredited and driven into exile; the rest were either deceivers or were deceived.[6]

That single paragraph declaring that there was a "temporary suspense" of the authority of the hierarchy during the Arian dispute especially enraged his critics, and he was called at one point "the most dangerous man in England." Under pressure from the Vatican he clarified his words by saying he did not mean to suggest the body of the bishops lost its mandate for a time, but that it failed for those many years in providing any "authoritative utterance" to untangle the combatants. And he marvels that though "the fourth century is the age of doctors, illustrated, as it was, by the saints, Athanasius, Hilary, the two Gregories, Basil, Chrysostom, Jerome and Augustine, and all of these saints...nevertheless in that very day, the divine tradition committed to the infallible church was proclaimed and maintained far more by the faithful than by the Episcopate."[7]

I could not help but wonder who these "faithful" were. Given the mass communications limitations of the fourth century, there could have hardly been an organized pan-Christendom campaign to "defend consubstantiality." The movement would have had to come independently from many directions, from Christian communities in all those diverse cities and regions, many of which don't exist anymore. And who were the leaders? They were undoubtedly laity with strong convictions; none of their names have been preserved, except for a few mentioned in the recorded anecdotes. What compelled them to prefer death rather than acknowledge the Arian iota? We will never know.

In this book and others Newman provides some insight. This powerful sense of the faithful springs, he speculates, from a kind of instinct for the truth residing in the body of the church and serving as an antibody, rejecting inauthentic teaching just as a physical body produces defenses against infection. In his analysis, doctrine, including infallible doctrine, can never be a top-down, one-way-street kind of enterprise. This doesn't mean there necessarily should exist a state of permanent conflict between the teaching church and the believing church. Rather, says Newman, they should function together in a kind of *conspiratio,* by which he doesn't mean a conspiracy, as the word has come to mean in modern English. He appeals to the original, literal meaning of the word in Latin, that is, breathing together.

As a general rule, says Newman, it is to be assumed that the teaching church, the so-called magisterium, and the believing church "breathe together" and in harmony. But as the ruckus after Nicaea indicates, situations can arise when the believing church does not accept, receive, or recognize as authentic what the bishops (or pope) are putting forth. Then it is imperative, in Newman's view, that the two sides work together for a return to healthy breathing. This requires, he thinks, patient listening by both sides to "the tradition of the Apostles" as it

> manifests itself variously at various times: sometimes by the mouth of the episcopacy, sometimes by the doctors [of the church], sometimes by the people, sometimes by liturgies, rites, ceremonies, and customs, by events, disputes, movements, and all those other phenomena which are comprised under the name of history. It follows that none of these channels of tradition may be treated with disrespect.

As for his own preference among the channels, Newman says, "I am accustomed to lay stress on the *consensus fidelium*."[8]

He adds that this should not short-circuit the role of the teaching church, which has the principal responsibility for wading cautiously, prayerfully, and with open mind through the tangle of sources and with open ear to what the Holy Spirit may be trying to say about resolving the dispute.

Newman's analysis and insights have crept into the works of many theologians, and he continues to be a catalyst for challenging ideas. For me his work was an eye-opener; I spent a lot of time poring though history and finding examples of people from many centuries who challenged the institutional church on a variety of issues, some of them doctrines that had been presented as irreversible. In one way or other, like the fourth-century faithful, they made their voice known concerning decisions of importance. All of them, Newman included, got in trouble for their efforts, and the great majority were later vindicated or somehow were erased from the history books. So I am convinced that the instinct for the truth Newman speaks of has always been operative in the church. Another name for it, I think, is the Holy Spirit.

Chapter Four

Control from Above, Participation from Below

————— ✝ —————

Early Christian texts are filled with a sense of community meetings, community sharing, community participation in decisions, and a strong belief that the consensus of the Christian people indicates the guidance of the Holy Spirit.
— Brian Tierney

I N 1996 Bishop Fabian Bruskewitz excommunicated from the church any Catholics in his Lincoln, Nebraska, diocese who dared to join Call to Action, a liberal organization of some twenty thousand, which questioned the official church position on certain doctrines. There were no preparatory hearings on the subject, no warning to the public, and no right of appeal. Bruskewitz provided no explanation other than to call Call to Action an "anti-Catholic cult." In more than a decade since that action, no other bishop in the United States has followed Bruskewitz's lead, nor has any bishop publicly chided Bruskewitz. Members of the organization appealed to the Vatican but heard nothing until a high-ranking Vatican cardinal in 2006 assured Bruskewitz he had acted within his authority. The case is still under appeal.

As a longtime member of Call to Action, I was indignant and angry. How could a bishop make himself judge, jury, and executioner without suffering consequences himself? How could he act in open contradiction of modern ideas of the right to a fair hearing — ideas that are basic to Catholic social teaching? The answer, of course, is that Bishop Bruskewitz was operating out of an authoritarian mind-set that developed in the church over many centuries. It was created out of historical conflicts between church and state, internal conflicts within the church itself, and a determination by church leaders to preserve order, no matter what the cost! It was a mind-set Dostoyevsky's Grand Inquisitor would have endorsed because, as he stated so eloquently, humans are "weak, vicious, worthless and rebellious" and cannot tolerate the gift of freedom.

It is a mind-set regarded by many church leaders today as obsolete and counterproductive in the long run. But some of its provisions are still on the books. Catholic bishops, all of whom within their own dioceses are answerable only to the pope, are theoretically free to exercise those provisions. Bishop Bruskewitz then could best be viewed as a model medieval ecclesiastic — a designation he might even be proud of.

The evolution of papal authority (and, by analogy, all church authority), from Peter in the first century with his commission to feed the sheep, to Boniface VIII in the fourteenth century and his self-declared power over all humanity, and to popes beyond, is incredibly complex. It is a story of a gradual curtailment of religious liberties and the right of free expression in a society that was always fearful of enemies from without and within. Yet to read the saga of the church exclusively from this vantage point is to miss the intellectual and cultural developments that were occurring beneath the radar of most historians. In towns and cities, later in universities, the lived, highly participative experience of the Catholic people was germinating ideas about individual rights, representative government, and constitutional guarantees. In time these ideas would blossom into the ideals of equality and democracy that would shape the modern world, though their creation in the womb of the medieval Catholic world would be largely forgotten.

To get a perspective on all this, I think it's helpful first to consider two popes, both named Gregory, who lived four hundred years apart. They illustrate the pressures the church experienced in very different eras, as well as the direction in which church leadership was moving in response to constant challenge.

Gregory I: A Non-Monarchical Vision

Gregory I served as pope from 590 to 604 CE, some two hundred years after the Council of Constantinople effectively ended the Arian controversy. Three other major councils had also been held during that period, at Ephesus, Chalcedon, and a second at Constantinople, all dealing with further disputes about the person and nature of Jesus. But now in the last years of the sixth century, pressing civil problems had to be dealt with. Barbarian attacks had taken a toll throughout the Roman Empire, which was entering its twilight years.

The aristocracy was broken, provincial governments were weak, so the bishops and popes were compelled to undertake responsibilities like negotiating treaties and providing cities with defenses against attacks. Gregory proved to be the right man for such tasks. He had in fact been trained in the art of politics as a young man and attained the rank of prefect of the City of Rome (a post roughly equivalent to that of mayor) while still in his twenties. He gave up a political career after a short time, established a monastery in his family's residence, and was ordained a deacon. Recognizing his talents, Pope Pelagius II sent him to Constantinople as his personal representative. Six years later the pope died and Gregory returned, finding himself quickly elected as Pelagius's successor.

During his fourteen-year reign, he was roundly praised as a masterful administrator in both church and state affairs. In the absence of competent civil leadership, he established the papacy as the de facto civil ruler of Italy, and he gradually came to be recognized as the primary bishop of the entire Western church. Nevertheless, he managed to exhibit a style of leadership remarkably close to the one Jesus recommended to his followers. He was the originator of the papal appellation "servant of the servants of the Lord," and the record indicates he was one pope who lived by it. He is also one of only two popes in history to be called "the Great," the other being Leo I in the mid-fifth century. Gregory placed special emphasis on the teaching of the first four great councils of the church. They should be "accepted like the four Gospels," he said, not because of his authority as pope, but because "they were established by the universal consent" of both clergy and laity.[1]

Among his achievements, Gregory urged the bishops of the West to hold regular local synods to work out their own problems. He greatly expanded the missionary outreach of the church, sending monks to England and other Anglo-Saxon areas. By careful diplomacy he forged a friendly relationship with the newly converted Visigoths in Spain and set the stage for the eventual conversion of the Lombards in Gaul. As testified by the more than 850 letters of Gregory that have survived, he accomplished all this with a remarkable combination of gentleness and appeal to common sense. I find interesting the choice of verbs historians use in describing Gregory's various interactions with bishops and civil leaders; invariably he "implored," "urged," "begged," "recommended," "discussed," or "persuaded."

For example, when he exhorted an elderly Numidian bishop to take steps to upgrade the qualifications for the priesthood, he wrote, "When therefore the council you are taking measures to assemble has, with the succor of God, been brought to a conclusion, gladden us by telling of its unity and concord, and give us information on all points."[2] When a Spanish archbishop expressed concern that in some places converts were being baptized by triple immersion in water instead of the traditional single immersion, Gregory responded that there were good reasons for both practices and both should be left in place. "Diversity of customs in the church does not impede unity of faith," he said.

He is also known for his concern about the rise of anti-Semitism; he forbade the forced conversion of Jews and established the pope as officially the "protector of the Jews."

Gregory was especially sensitive to the feelings of estrangement the Eastern churches were feeling toward Rome. When several bishops began referring to him in correspondence as the "universal bishop," he wrote to one, "Let not your Holiness in your epistles ever call anyone universal, lest you detract from the honor due to yourself in offering to another what is not his due."[3] To another bishop he wrote, "I consider nothing to be an honor to me through which my brothers lose the honor that is their due."[4] He was equally concerned that the Eastern patriarchs similarly refrain from labeling themselves or their positions as "universal." To John the Faster of Constantinople, who titled himself the "universal and ecumenical patriarch," he said, "If then [Paul the Apostle] shunned subjecting certain members of Christ to particular apostles . . . what will you say to Christ . . . in the last judgment, having . . . put all His members under yourself by the appellation of universal?"[5] In his writings, most notably "Pastoral Rule," he placed the essence of ministry in personal service, not in the acquisition of control or honors.

According to historian William La Due, Gregory's "thoughts reflect a vision which was clearly not monarchical. He saw the five patriarchs as the regional heads of the Church, and for him it seems the five were on something of an equal footing, with no one of them exercising a universal jurisdiction over the others."[6] Gregory the Great is an excellent example of the communitarian style of leadership that marked much of the first millennium. Nothing stays the same forever. In the years following Gregory I, popes would begin operating out of very different visions.

Gregory VII: Reform through Control

The other Gregory, Gregory VII, also known by his family name, Hildebrand, was pope from 1073 to 1085, some 470 years after the first Gregory. The two are sometimes confused in historical accounts because both were so prominent in their times and left behind such substantial records. Like his namesake, Gregory VII has admirers, some regarding him as "the greatest who ever sat in Peter's chair."[7] He is the central figure in the often cited Gregorian Reform, which set the church on a path that continues to this day. And for that reason, he also has harsh critics who see him as the father of serious problems that still afflict the church today. This Gregory is in many ways exemplary of the authoritarian style of leadership that would mark the second millennium.

The styles and visions of the two Gregories were so different, it is difficult to remember they held the same position. Whereas historians speak of Gregory I as imploring, urging, and even begging in his communications, the verbs repeatedly chosen for Gregory VII's papal actions are more likely to be "threatened," "warned," "accused," "confronted," "prohibited," and "excommunicated."

Hildebrand was elected pope in the midst of a titanic struggle between church and state. The prestige and power that Gregory I deftly exercised, centuries before in the Holy Roman Empire, had collapsed. Civil authorities not only ran civil governments; they now ran the church as well. The ancient practice of bishops being elected by the clergy with the approval of the people had disappeared. In its place stood a new system in which bishops and popes were appointed by the royal elite — a system often identified by one of its characteristics, "lay investiture." Notes historian Thomas Bokenkotter:

> The dominance of the Church by lay power was true not only in Germany. Everywhere in Europe the feudal potentates were applying...the same kind of system, using the Church as they saw fit.... The bishop-to-be knelt before the lord, rendered him homage and fealty, and received from him his staff and ring. The land and attached jurisdiction also conferred on him...were regarded as a fief, whose feudal obligations took precedence over ecclesiastical ones. The whole transaction was tainted with simony besides,

since the new bishop ordinarily paid a heavy fee for his promotion.[8]

Priests were also widely involved in the system, often passing on their parish fiefdoms to their offspring or other relatives.

Efforts had been made earlier in the eleventh century to revive papal authority, notably through the use of the largely forged Pseudo-Isadorian Decretals, which attributed to ancient popes authority over the whole church that they never had claimed. A requirement of permanent celibacy was imposed on all priests, and the church dissolved the marriages of those active priests who had wives. In 1059 a papal proclamation excluded emperors, kings, and other royalty from involvement in the choice or appointment of popes and bishops. The royalty rose up in immediate protest of the proclamation, and it appeared for a time that their will would prevail. Then came Hildebrand.

He had been an archdeacon in the papal curia, a man who wielded authority with almost frightening self-assurance. He was, according to accounts of the day, "small in stature, weak in voice, only moderately learned," but he had the fiery temperament of an Old Testament prophet and drew men to him by the vigor of his imagination, the bright keenness of his eyes and his tremendous passion for righteousness."[9] As pope, he hurled himself into the effort to end lay control of the church wherever it could be found.

Typical of his style as pope is a letter he wrote to the archbishop of Bremen, who had disagreed with him. Gregory called him an "enemy" and said,

> You placed every possible hindrance in the way of our legate... and when you were summoned to Rome you failed to appear. Wherefore we summon and order you to present yourself [in Rome]... in the first week of the coming Lent for... correction.... In consequence of the above mentioned offenses we suspend you from all Episcopal functions until you appear before us.[10]

Gregory's vision of the papal power went well beyond that of his predecessors. He saw the church as not only necessarily independent and supreme in its own domain but also as exercising supremacy in civil matters too. In a document called "Dictates of the Pope," he listed twenty-seven statements about the juridical rights of the papacy. Among them:

"The Roman pontiff alone is rightly to be called universal";

he "alone can depose or reinstate bishops";

his legate, "even if of lower grade, takes precedence in a council over all the bishops";

he "alone may depose emperors";

no sentence of his "may be retracted by anyone";

the Roman Church "has never erred, nor ever shall err to all eternity."[11]

These dictates would be taken seriously by popes and even added to in the centuries ahead.

Gregory's best-known battle was with the emperor, Henry IV of Germany. When Gregory attempted to enforce the ban on lay control, Henry contradicted him by investing his own choice as bishop of Milan, declaring, "Hildebrand is not pope but false monk" and ordering him to "descend and be damned throughout the ages!" Gregory swiftly excommunicated Henry and deposed him as emperor. Shocked by the pope's action, most of Henry's supporters deserted him. Momentarily repentant, Emperor Henry, with his wife, infant son, and a handful of supporters, climbed the Alps in early 1077 to the town of Canossa where the pope was staying. When Gregory refused to see him, Henry stood barefoot in the snow for three days until Gregory relented and gave him absolution.

Henry and his retinue returned home, but he had hardly warmed his feet when he became involved in another dispute with the pope, who promptly re-excommunicated him. Henry retaliated by attacking Rome with an army, Gregory barely escaping into exile. But papal supporters finally drove Henry out of Rome, leaving much of the city in ruins as a result. The people of Rome blamed Gregory for the damage and prevented his return. Gregory VII died, feeling himself a failure. His final words: "I have loved justice and hated iniquity; therefore I die in exile."[12]

His efforts and example, however, profoundly affected the church. Lay involvement in the selection of bishops would be seriously circumscribed in the centuries to come, and eventually so was direct clergy involvement. More and more decision making on church matters would become centralized in Rome, as papal power was extolled over every other consideration. The papacy would become a true monarchy, freely exercising religious authority and effectively claiming jurisdiction even in civil affairs. Not surprisingly, the triumphalistic attitude proved contagious. It came to be imitated in the self-regard and public display of many bishops and more than a few priests as they basked in their shared powers with the pope. Here is Pope Innocent III, a hundred years after Gregory VII:

> You see then who is this servant set over the household, successor of Peter, anointed of the Lord . . . set between God and man, lower than God but higher than man, who judges all and is judged by no one.[13]

And here is Boniface VIII, two hundred years after Gregory:

> There are two swords in the control of the Church, the temporal and the spiritual . . . but the latter is used for the Church and the former by the Church. One is used by the hand of the priest, the other by the hands of kings and knights at the command and with the permission of the priest. . . . We therefore declare, say, affirm and announce that for every human creature submission to the Roman pontiff is absolutely necessary for salvation.[14]

Though he did not live to see it, the creation of classic medieval Christendom may be appropriately credited to — or blamed on — Gregory VII.

The Origins of a Democratic Church

Steeped in the ideals of individual freedom and American democracy, I was troubled, like most Catholics educated in the late twentieth century, by this rise of papal absolutism. Was this the end of the story? Did no one protest? Did everyone roll over and accept this top-down interpretation of church as God's will for all time? Certainly there were indications that this was the case in the adulation of hierarchy in Catholic schools and Catholic popular culture. And indications of it persist in this new century in lingering abuses of clericalism and the occasional hurling of ecclesiastical lightning bolts by hierarchs like Bishop Bruskewitz.

But I have learned that a totally different way of understanding the church and its operation was developing apart from the rigid papal model, even when the authoritarian spirit prevailed in both church and state. In 1140, just fifty-five years after the death of Gregory VII, there appeared an amazing publication called the "Concord of Discordant Canons" or *Decretum* for short. The compiler of this immense work was a man named Gratian, about whom little is known except that he must have had an obsessive-compulsive nature and a fanatical dedication to put things in rational order. Gratian, generally considered the father of canon law, had pulled together the rules and regulations, the canons and decrees from the church's twelve-hundred-year history, from ancient councils and synods, from the writings of popes and church fathers. Not only did he put this mass of material in readable volumes, he tried to make sense of it all, to show the consistencies and inconsistencies in the church from the beginning. In this he failed. But what he did leave as legacy was a kind of archaeological mound for scholars and canon lawyers to dig through for the next four centuries. A new profession of "decretists" and canonists emerged. They had names like Hugucchio, Johannes Teutonicus, and Alanus. From their excavations in this mound and aided by the renewed interest in old Roman law, they began to put together a comprehensive view of how the church functioned in the past and how it might function in the future. Equally important, they produced fresh, compelling ideas on how any society, religious or secular, ought to work for the good of all its members.

You will find scant mention of these decretists or their work in popular history books. The one scholar I encountered who has made this work intelligible to modern readers is the prolific historian of the medieval world, Brian Tierney. In scores of articles and books he opened the door to these figures from the dim past who were trying to find some workable middle ground between the absolutist mind-set of the official church of their day and the varied mind-sets of Christians who came before. To be sure, they could find evidence in the *Decretum* of top-down, monarchical claims of the hierarchy. But they found other, intriguing strains of thought. Says Tierney:

> Early Christian texts are filled with a sense of community meetings, community sharing, community participation in decisions, and above all they reflect a strong belief that the consensus of the Christian people indicates the guidance of the Holy Spirit in the church.... Whatever power prelates possessed in the early church, they possessed it on behalf of their communities and as representing their communities.[15]

The decretists noted how Cyprian of Carthage depended on the agreement of the community for his major decisions, how Gregory I founded the authority of the first four ecumenical councils on the "universal consent" of clergy and laity, how Augustine held that when Peter accepted from Jesus the "keys," he did so as a symbol or representative of the whole church. They developed ideas on ways in which the pope's sovereignty could be reconciled with the fact that he was human too, that he could err, had in fact erred in the past, and on occasion had even been deposed. They speculated that a general council might serve as a check and balance on papal power.

The decretists took seriously the old Roman adage, "What touches all must be approved by all," meaning that everyone who will be affected by a decision deserves to have a voice in that decision. They contended that laity, as a general rule, should be therefore invited to church councils since matters of belief and doctrine "touch" their lives. For the first time scholars analyzed and dissected the great pantheon of juridical concepts that had been used and abused over the centuries — ideas like power, authority, jurisdiction, rights, obligations, consent. They wrote about corporations as fictional persons that have a legal existence separate from that of the corporate members, about individual rights and the protections of these rights in conflicts. The critical idea that came up over and over in their commentaries and glosses was the full consent of the people. They saw it as crucial in communities, secular or religious, and they found representative governments, founded on constitutions, as the singular way that the consent of a people could be guaranteed. Obviously, these scholars were searching for ways to protect the community from authoritarianism. They could see no other way to do this than by a broad participation of the people in many levels of church government, including the highest level.

One might be tempted to regard all this effort as idle speculation by a group of isolated intellectuals. In fact, the record shows their ideas were infiltrating the Catholic Church in a variety of ways. According to church law, a bishop had his cathedral chapter of canons, a group of men who elected him. "Typically bishop and canons ruled the church together," says Tierney. "A major act involving the welfare of the whole church required the assent of both parties, the bishop and the majority of the canons."[16] It was a type of corporation in which the bishop was considered the principal member and chief agent, but his authority was checked and balanced by the necessary assent of the canons, resulting in a limited, monarchical form of government.

When Innocent III (he of the "lower than God but higher than man" self-description) summoned the Fourth Lateran Council in 1213, he felt compelled to announce it would be "representative" of the whole church, and it was. The four hundred bishops, eight hundred abbots, plus representatives of college churches and cathedral chapters, envoys of kings and major cities (most of whom were laymen) constituted the greatest assembly ever of the Western church. The broad representation made it possible for the council to pass important reform legislation.

Also in the thirteenth century, the newly founded Dominican order put in place a complex representative system with enough checks and balances to foil the plans of any overly ambitious superior. Thomas Aquinas, the great Dominican theologian of that time, was also influenced by the new ideas. He contradicted the old argument that monarchy was the best form of government since it imitated God's rule over all creation. Instead, said Thomas, a mixed constitutional form seemed preferable because that is what God gave the Jews in the book of Exodus — with Moses as a kind of king, the seventy-two elders acting as an oligarchy, and the people who directly chose the elders forming a democracy. He did not go so far as to suggest that the church might operate in the same way — with the pope as monarch, the cardinals as oligarchy, and the bishops (chosen by the people) as the democratic element. But others did, citing Aquinas as their source. According to Tierney:

> By maintaining that the democratic element in a constitution consisted in the right of a people to elect its rulers, Thomas had, in effect, turned the old idea of a mixed constitution into an argument, grounded in both secular and scriptural sources, that could explain and justify the growth of representative institutions in church and state.[17]

As it turned out, the new ideas found a more welcome and permanent home in the state than in the church. The principle, "What touches all must be approved by all," was applied to the government of the Italian communes in the fifteenth century and eventually became a guiding argument for free elections in many regions. Most history books find the origins of modern democracy in the writings of seventeenth-century philosophers like John Locke and Thomas Hobbes. Their contributions were indeed significant, but there is clear evidence that the origins of these modern ideas can be found in the insights of the Catholic decretists and canonists some four hundred years earlier. Ironically, the institutional church did not embrace those ideas in its own structure and for a long time opposed their implementation in the secular world as well. Observes Tierney:

> The modern practices of representation and consent that characterize secular constitutional government are not alien to the tradition of the church. And if in the future the church should choose to adopt such practices to meet its own needs in a changing world, that would not be a revolutionary departure but a recovery of a lost part of the church's own early tradition.[18]

I believe the time is ripe for such a recovery.

Chapter Five

Conciliarism:
Resistance to Papal Supremacy

———— ✝ ————

This sacred synod... declares that all men of every rank and position, including the pope himself, are bound to obey it in those matters that pertain to the faith, the removal of ... schism, and the reformation of the Church in head and members. — COUNCIL OF CONSTANCE

F EW THINGS SPEAK TO ME more starkly of the disappointments of history than the Council of Constance, a fifteenth-century ecumenical gathering of the bishops that had enormous potential. It might have been a turning point — an opening to a broader participation of the People of God in the church. For a time that's what it seemed to have achieved, in addition to the immediate problem it solved. But in the end the long-range hopes it built up floundered. Almost as disappointing is the virtual disappearance of the council from the memory of Christianity. If it is mentioned at all in Catholic history books, it's presented as a minor glitch — a hiccup — along the way. The Council of Constance has been reinterpreted, reassessed, and explained away so successfully that it is seen today, if at all, as an irrelevancy. When I took the time several years ago to examine the record of this unique event, I was instantly reminded of a central theme in George Orwell's novel *1984*:

> The Party could thrust its hand into the past and say of this or that, it never happened. The Party said that Oceania had

never been in alliance with Eurasia. He, Winston Smith, knew that Oceania had been in alliance with Eurasia as short a time as four years ago. But where did that knowledge exist? Only in his own consciousness, which in any case must be soon annihilated. And if all others accepted the lie which the party imposed — if all the records told the same tale — then the lie passed into history and became the truth. "Who controls the past," ran the party slogan, "controls the future: who controls the present controls the past."[1]

In the case of Constance no single "party" recast history. The transformation was a joint effort carried out over the centuries by popes and cardinals and priests, by educators and catechists and church apologists who did not want to discuss an embarrassing possibility: If the Council of Constance had worked, the Protestant Reformation might not have occurred.

The Appeal of Conciliarism

The concept at the heart of Constance was an idea called conciliarism. In essence it is the conviction that the ultimate focus of authority resides in the whole body of the church, not exclusively in its papal head; it declares that under certain circumstances a general council representing the full church can exercise authority apart from the pope, even in opposition to him. If such an idea were seriously proposed today, it would elicit emphatic denials; it would be seen as a near blasphemous denial of the church's true essence. Yet conciliarism had a respectable life in Christianity for centuries. It was discussed and debated in universities. It was seen by many Catholics as a restraint on the absolutist claims of more than a few medieval popes and a potential answer to the grave abuses that threatened the church. Everyone knew about excessive church taxation, the buying and selling of church offices, the scandalous lives of many clergy. They knew too that real reform would not be authorized or implemented if the church's one head remained indifferent or totally preoccupied with pressing political and fiscal problems.

Ideas about general councils were first generated in the twelfth and thirteenth centuries when decretists like Hugucchio, following up on Gratian's collection, examined the notions of jurisdiction, representation, and consent (discussed in chapter 4). They conceived of the church as a corporation, with its power lying not just in its head but diffused also in its members. Thomas Aquinas's ideas about governments with mixed constitutions, that is, having at one and the same time monarchic, aristocratic, and democratic components providing needed checks and balances, were further developed in the fourteenth century by prominent canonists and theologians like Marsilius of Padua, William of Ockham, and Hervaeus Natalis, master general of the Dominican Order. The church's general councils, with their proven record of providing direction and ending disputes, seemed the logical vehicle for embodying some of these ideas — if councils could operate with a greater sense of true authority. None of these prominent forerunners of conciliarism were accused of proposing dangerous theories, nor were its later outspoken advocates charged with heresy. The theories were alive in the public consciousness and were published and discussed without fear of censure.

By the fifteenth century conciliarism came in three varieties. The first and mildest called for "periodic and frequent" assemblies of general councils, with little mention of how they would operate vis-à-vis the pope. The second planned for the cardinals to function as a kind of ongoing council, limiting papal supremacy by requiring the pope to seek their advice, direction, and consent. The third, called strict conciliarism, is the most important since it was operative at the Council of Constance. According to historian Francis Oakley, it is:

> the belief that the pope, however divinely-instituted his office, was not an absolute monarch but in some sense a constitutional ruler; that he possessed a ... ministerial

authority delegated to him by the community of the faithful for the good of the whole Church; that that community had not exhausted its inherent authority in the mere act of electing its ruler but had retained whatever residual power was necessary to prevent its own subversion or destruction; that it could exercise that power via its representatives assembled in a general council, could do so in certain critical cases even against the wishes of the pope and, in such cases, could proceed if need be to judge, chastise and even depose the pope.[2]

And just at this time in the fifteenth century the church found itself in a state of utter paralysis that it had never before experienced. It appeared to many that here was an ideal test case for the conciliar idea. To explain how the church got into this bizarre predicament, here is a capsulized chronology of the two-hundred-year roots of the problem:

- In 1305 Pope Clement V, under pressure from the French king, Philip the Fair, moved the entire papal operation to Avignon, a city known for its mild climate, in the south of France. He and his successors stayed — for seventy-two years — exhausting the papal treasury in a lavish and corrupt lifestyle and offending the people of Christendom. Meanwhile, wars raged in the papal states and the Black Death ravaged whole cities and depopulated countless monasteries and convents.

- In 1377 Pope Gregory XI, under the influence of Catherine of Siena, broke the French stranglehold on the papacy, closed down the Avignon facilities, and returned to Rome, thus ending what had been termed "the Babylonian Captivity of the Church."

- The next year, 1378, riot conditions prevailed in Rome during the election of a new pope. The people of Rome made clear by death threats and other measures that they would not tolerate another French pope, who just might take off for Avignon; they demanded an Italian pope. And they got one when the cardinals elected Urban VI. However, the cardinals soon after fled Rome for France and announced that the election was invalid due to their fear of the Roman mobs. They then elected a new pope, Clement VII, who, to no one's surprise, set up headquarters in (yes) Avignon. This marked the beginning of what is called "the Great Western Schism." The governments of Christendom split their allegiances, half supporting Urban and his successors and half backing Clement and his. This unhappy situation persisted for another thirty-one years and then got worse.

- Since no one knew who the real pope was, a general council was finally assembled in Pisa, Italy, in 1409, drawing a large representation of bishops, other clerics, theologians, and ambassadors of most nations. They did not invoke the doctrine of conciliarism but in effect used the strict interpretation of it. "Never shall we succeed in ending the schism," said the council members, "while these two obstinate persons are at the head of the opposing parties."[3] With near unanimity the council deposed both popes and declared the chair of St. Peter vacant. The cardinals then elected a new pope, who promptly died. His elected successor was Pope John XXIII (not to be confused with the "other" John XXIII of the twentieth century). The decision was hailed universally throughout the church and at the major universities. The schism, it seemed, was over. But it wasn't. The two deposed popes refused to step down. The result: three popes, one representing the Roman line started by Urban VI, one representing a French line started by Clement VII, and one representing the new Pisa line — each claiming to be the sole pope and each waging war and hurling insults at the others. Historians wonder how the faith of pious Christians survived. Thus was the scene set for the Council of Constance.

Soon after his election John XXIII showed his true colors. In his previous life he had been a showboating military leader, who was described as personally corrupt and a "zero in moral and spiritual matters." As pope he appointed relatives to high posts, spent papal funds on self-promotional projects, and alienated most of his cardinals and curia officials. It became obvious that the desperately needed reforms would never happen with him in charge. Leading theologians and churchmen of the day, Nicholas of Cusa, Cardinal Francesco Zabarella, Pierre D'Ailley, and Jean Gerson, chancellor of the University of Paris, all proponents of conciliarism, were in the forefront, pressing for a council with teeth, one that could get permanent results.

Sigismund of Lithuania, the newly elected Holy Roman Emperor, stepped in and persuaded John to convene another general council. It officially opened in 1414, five years after Pisa, in the city of Constance, on the border of Germany and present-day Switzerland. When Pope John arrived in style, riding a white horse, wearing gold-studded Mass vestments, and leading a procession of his cardinals and attendants, it appeared that most of Christendom was already present or on the way. Reports on the actual attendance are unreliable, but writers who were there concurred it was by far the largest ecclesiastical aggregation of participants and onlookers in the history of the church. One report listed as present patriarchs, 29 cardinals, 33 archbishops, 500 bishops, 100 abbots, 300 theologians, and 18,000 other clerics, plus an outpouring of the faithful beyond all counting. They came by horseback and mule, in carriages, wagons, and carts, and on foot, some from hundreds of miles away. It was said in one account that 36,000 beds had to be brought into the city to accommodate the multitude — two to a bed.

I could not find in the literature on Constance any explanations for the size of the throng, but I would venture that this was nothing less than a medieval manifestation of the sense of the faithful. Ordinary Christians were disgusted by the repeated failures to reform; they wanted the assembly to know it was time for meaningful change; their presence here represented perhaps more a threat than a plea.

In the early sessions Gerson and Zabarella argued for — and got — a new form of voting which would counter John XXIII's

efforts to rig the voting by bringing with him a large assortment
of bishops he had himself appointed. When he observed the grim,
serious mood of the council members, John realized there was
little chance he would survive as pope. So he secretly fled Constance disguised as a groom. The council set to work, operating,
with apparently no objection, on the principles of conciliarism,
with which all were now familiar. Lest there be any question
about their intent or legitimacy, they declared in the fourth and
fifth sessions that all popes — not just the three claimants — are
subordinate to general councils of the church. The decree *Haec
sancta* is quite explicit:

> This sacred synod of Constance . . . declares in the first place
> that it forms a general council representing the Catholic
> Church, that it has its power immediately from Christ, and
> that all men of every rank and position, including the pope
> himself, are bound to obey it in those matters that pertain
> to the faith, the removal of . . . schism, and to the reforma-
> tion of the Church in head and members. It declares also
> that anyone of any rank, condition or office — even the
> papal — who shall persistently refuse to obey the mandates,
> statutes, decrees, or instructions made by this holy synod
> or by any other lawfully assembled council on the mat-
> ters aforesaid or on things pertaining to them, shall, unless
> he recovers his senses, be subjected to fitting penance and
> punished as is appropriate.[4]

In a second decree, *Frequens,* future popes were ordered to
convene general councils at specified, regular intervals, usually
every ten years. Meanwhile, the pope in the Roman line, Gregory XII, appeared at the council and presented his resignation,
whereupon he was honored and allowed to sit in the presider's
seat. The claimant in the Avignon line, Benedict XIII, never appeared at the council. He fled to a fortress and was deposed at
a later session of the council. John XXIII was apprehended and
brought to the council, where he was tried for notorious simony,

abetting schism, and leading a scandalous life; he too chose to resign.

With the papacy now officially vacant, the council authorized the election of a new pope. The winner, in November 1417, was a respected Italian bishop who took the name Martin V. According to the records of the time, this settlement was universally received in the Christian world, just as Pisa had been at first. But this time there were no claims of illegality and no further resistance from the backers of the three ousted former claimants. Still, the papal issues (and the condemnation of several heretics) consumed so much time and energy that the council never got around to the problem of genuine reform, which, in fact, had been the underlying reason for the pressure to end the schism in the first place.

But at least the Great Western Schism was over and a single, unopposed pope would take up residence in Rome after almost forty years of turmoil. The conciliar theory had not only won the day; it was the official doctrine of the Catholic Church, authorized by the declaration of a general council. Claims of papal absolutism would be tempered by the restraints of shared authority. Through regular councils the church would become a more constitutional, collegial, deliberative, discerning institution. Gradually, the new approach would trickle down into the operations of the church's bishops, into the lower clergy, even into the far-flung parishes of Christendom. Such was the hope of leaders like Gerson and D'Ailley who had paved the way.

Confusion and Havoc

The euphoria proved premature. When Martin V got to Rome, he was overwhelmed with the wretched conditions of the papal states and the city. It was said that wolves roamed the streets. The pope became so involved in rallying military and civil forces to confront the catastrophes that he gave scant attention to the need for church reform. Nor was he particularly interested in convoking a council, since the new arrangement decreed at Constance had not been tested with a sitting pope. His successor, Eugene IV, was even less enthusiastic about the arrangement. However, under pressure from leading clergy and laity, he did summon a council at Basel in present-day Switzerland in 1431. From the start Eugene's concerns were justified; the proceedings went badly. Some supporters of conciliarism began to interpret the Constance decision as confining the pope to a totally secondary status and elevating the general council to the level of supremacy. After a time he issued a bull dissolving the council. But the attendees at Basel defied the order and went ahead with business without him.

As more and more bishops arrived at the council and more governments supported its legitimacy on the basis of the Constance decree, Eugene withdrew the bull and recognized the council's rights without reservation. Nevertheless, the radical fringe of the gathering continued to operate almost as if the pope did not exist, strongly reaffirming *Haec sancta* and passing extreme reform legislation that would deprive the pope of the right to tax the clergy. Oakley said the members "moved beyond their predecessors at Constance and edged into somewhat more radical territory.... They turned from notions of mixed monarchy and divided sovereignty to that of community sovereignty, [that is] an unlimited jurisdiction...to the Church-in-council, with the pope as merely its executive servant."[5]

Eugene saw a way out of this problem when the Eastern Byzantine Church, separated from papal jurisdiction for almost four hundred years, indicated interest in reunion with the West. If that could be achieved, the papal reputation would be greatly restored. To facilitate discussions Eugene called for the council to move its deliberations to Ferrara in Italy. But the majority at Basel refused to move, while a minority went with the pope. When negotiations with Eastern Church representatives went surprisingly well at Ferrara and it appeared there might indeed be a reunion of all Christianity, many bishops deserted Basel and joined the pope.

In July 1439, amid great rejoicing, the reunion became official, with the Eastern representatives accepting the pope as head of the universal church and vicar of Christ. By this unexpected success, Pope Eugene turned the tables on the Basel assembly and undermined the whole conciliar idea in the popular mind. But the reunion proved stillborn. When the Byzantine churchmen returned home, the public staunchly refused to embrace the decision, thereby providing an example of the rejection of a doctrine by a body of the Christian Church. Thus all the efforts at Ferrara proved in vain; to this day the Eastern and Western branches of the church remain unreconciled. The rump assembly at Basel held sessions for another four years until it was dissolved by order of the pope and emperor. As a result, the attempt to put the conciliar idea into practice ended in disaster. The Basel recommendations for reform were never taken seriously.

In the latter part of the fifteenth and the early part of the sixteenth centuries, the call for reform became more urgent. Simony, the sale of church positions, including the office of bishop or cardinal, to the highest bidder, had grown rampant. For example, Albrecht of Brandenburg bought the archbishop's seat in Mainz for ten thousand ducats and then raised the money he needed by promoting the sale of indulgences, with the cooperation of the curia. Kings and other royalty managed to get their sons appointed to high church posts, even though they lacked any qualifications. A whole population of priests appeared throughout Europe whose sole duty was to say Mass. Parish priests were poorly educated, the religious education of the young was largely ignored, and concubinage was common among the clergy. Appeals for a new council increased. But the popes, unwilling to face the unsettled state of conciliarism, ignored them. One pope in 1460 published a bull condemning these appeals, calling them "erroneous and detestable." Other pontiffs in 1483 and 1509 repeated the prohibition. The message for the better part of a century was, "Stop bothering us!"

When a group of bishops, disgusted by the delay, attempted
to summon a general council on their own, Pope Leo X finally
convoked the Fifth Lateran Council in 1512. Despite the pressure for effective reform, the assembly dragged on for five years
without accomplishing anything. The council decrees, said historian William La Due, "were characterized by timidity, and hence
nothing really came of them. Lateran V did not honestly and
courageously confront the needs of the church for thorough-
going reform in head and members."[6] It appeared both sides,
supporters of strict papal monarchy and backers of strict conciliarism, had run out of energy. In 1516 the council published
a bull that declared the pope has authority over all councils, including the right to convoke, transfer, and dissolve them; it did
not mention the conciliar theory. The next year, 1517, the Au-
gustinian monk Martin Luther nailed his ninety-five theses on
the church door at Wittenberg.

When the Protestant Reform hit Europe with hurricane force,
all subtleties were thrown to the wind. Church leaders agreed
on the need for strong leadership in the emergency — a single
commander-in-chief to restore order. The popes of that era
served dutifully in what was a wartime situation. The reform
of head and members was vigorously implemented; the hemorrhaging finally stopped. But the body of the church would
be thereafter split, and efforts to put it together have not been
successful.

I think it's fair to ask, "What if?" What if the conciliar theory had avoided the train wreck at Basel? What if Martin V
or Eugene IV or any of those popes who came after them decided to view the Constance decree as a new beginning? What if
they had sat down with the best theorists of conciliarism and the
best bishops and cardinals of the day to chart out a way for pope
and council to work collaboratively for the good of Catholicism,
with neither side overly protective of its assumptions? And what
if it had worked? Then those eighty-one years between Basel
and Lateran V might be remembered as a time of unique, Spirit-
driven creativity. "Cardinal" Luther might be remembered for

his leadership in implementing genuine reform throughout Germany. And the church in which we grew up would have been very different.

Having lost its way as a spearhead of change, conciliarism lived on for years in various mutations. It was occasionally embraced by kings or princes as a way to limit papal domination, most notably in France under the name of Gallicanism. And it was mentioned over the years by theologians as a possible way to solve doctrinal tussles with the Vatican. However, after the First Vatican Council in 1870 and its proclamation of the infallibility of the pope, conciliarism disappeared almost completely from the church's consciousness. And so did the councils of Pisa and Constance.

A Revised History

I am amazed at the power of creative redaction, by which events once thought to signify one thing are re-explained to signify something quite different or to signify nothing at all. The Council of Pisa, which was originally received by the church as the solution of the two-pope embarrassment, is not to be found on any list of general councils today. When mentioned at all, it is sometimes spoken of as a "schismatic council" inasmuch as it was not convoked by a certainly legitimate pope! Other times it is called partially schismatic and partially valid. For some years the Council of Constance also disappeared from the screen of authentic councils for the same reason, but it is now listed in most serious works as a true general council. Since it did, in fact, solve the three-pope embarrassment, it cannot be ignored.

But since Vatican I, much thought has gone into explaining that *Haec sancta,* the decree under which the Council of Constance operated, has no significance today. The most common dismissal is to call the decree "a time-bound emergency measure" that did not (and was not meant to) have any ongoing validity; it was created for a unique problem at a most dark moment in history, and, having used its power, expired for all time. Some eminent thinkers like historian Brian Tierney and theologian Francis Sullivan subscribe to versions of this view. The difficulty is that the wording of *Haec sancta* seems anything but time-bound. Phrases like "power from Christ" ... "matters that pertain to the faith" ... "all men of every rank including the pope himself" ... "persistently refuses to obey" ... "by this holy synod or by any other lawfully assembled Council" suggest absolute, permanent intent on the part of the framers of the decree. Nevertheless, Sullivan says, *Haec sancta* should be seen only as a valid "legislative decree" (and therefore of limited duration) but not as a dogma of faith with permanent validity in the church.[7]

Some explanations of Constance are entirely fanciful. One version declares that John XXIII, who was elected at Pisa, was really an "anti-pope," while the "true pope" at the council was Urban VI, who came late and graciously resigned his claim on the papacy. Since Urban was the true pope and was honored for his cooperation, goes the argument, everything approved before his arrival, including *Haec sancta,* had no validity. Therefore in this view Constance became a true general council only after Urban's arrival. This seems more like a legalistic loophole since it ignores what the people who were present and voting intended. If anyone there was a "true pope" in the minds of the council members, it was John XXIII. He was elected at Pisa, he convoked the Council of Constance, and he was formally deposed by the full council, largely for his immoral life and lack of cooperation. This is a crucial point because it was precisely under the provision of the conciliar decree that Constance disposed of two doubtful popes and deposed a third one.

Arguably then, conciliarism in one form or another is still alive, though in deep coma. And there are theologians like Francis Oakley and Hans Küng who refuse to regard it as "a dead issue, an ecclesiastical fossil, something lodged deep in the lower carboniferous of the dogmatic geology."[8] They think it an authentic piece of tradition that once served to preserve the church from self-destruction, and they believe it could be revived to serve again lest church authority ever become too unbalanced, too centralized. Besides that, some see in conciliar theory hints of how a church in tune with the Spirit of the New Testament ought to operate on a regular basis. Who controls the past, they believe, need not necessarily control the future.

Chapter Six

The American Experiment
in Democracy

---✝---

The idea of church as a clerical preserve was not part of the colonial heritage.... For this reason it would be much easier to graft the spirit of democracy onto the church during the period of reorganization. — JAY DOLAN

SEVERAL YEARS AGO I became obsessed with the story of the seventeenth-century Jesuit missionary Matteo Ricci. After he had entered the closed world of China, Ricci attempted to meld the basic truths of Christianity with the customs, traditions, and even the spiritual practices of the Chinese people. Ricci was convinced that there existed a certain compatibility between the two that might facilitate the spread of the gospel. The people's reverence for ancestors and parents, their concern for order in society, and their esteem of "loving kindness" as the highest of all virtues — all these struck Ricci as characteristics to build on. He thought what was already true and noble in Chinese culture might be grafted onto the Catholic faith. Ricci departed from missionary practice by dressing like the highly educated mandarin literati, learning the Chinese language, and not just studying the great books of Confucius but memorizing them!

I read everything I could find about Ricci and spent three weeks in China, where I found that four hundred years after his death and in this rigid, doctrinaire communist state, he is still remembered and venerated. I visited the place of his first church and the giant memorial stones erected in honor of Ricci and other Jesuits who came after him and continued to graft Catholicism onto the Chinese experience and culture. At one time, despite wars, persecutions, earthquakes, and growing concern by the Vatican, China reportedly held half a million Confucian Christians. The engagement officially ended in 1739 with a papal decree effectively forbidding the mingling of Catholicism with "pagan practices."

Ricci never used the term "inculturation," but that's exactly what he was doing. I attempted to write a book about him and his pioneering work. Now that inculturation is an accepted goal, at least theoretically, in the Catholic Church, it seemed to me there's much we could learn from this uniquely inventive man. However, I had to abandon the project, partly because I could not get inside Ricci's head, partly because I could not get the Chinese culture and mind-set inside my head, and largely because publishers did not believe a book on old history would sell. Only lately have I realized that inculturation was not unique to Ricci. Right here in the United States such an effort occurred just after the Revolution — a prolonged effort to graft the values and ideals of the democratic experience onto American Catholicism. We read about it in our Catholic history books but did not know what it was, maybe because it happened too close to home — and in its own determined way it is still going on.

Seizing the Opportunity

The Great Enlightenment in the eighteenth century with its emphasis on the preeminence of reason, the inevitability of human progress, and the rights of the individual affected the entire Western world. It led to the collapse of European monarchies, the American and French revolutions, and the birth of the modern world. Naturally the new thinking affected religion as well. And though Catholic Church leaders regarded Enlightenment ideas with extreme alarm, the ideas crept into the hearts and minds of

Catholics too and took root there. America proved an especially fertile ground.

At the time of the American Revolution the Catholic population was small, some twenty-five thousand mostly clustered in Maryland and Pennsylvania. There Catholics, who had long endured prejudice and discrimination from the Protestant majorities in the colonies, rejoiced in the events of 1776 and beyond, as full toleration gradually became the law of the land. According to historian Jay Dolan,

> When Catholics began to organize themselves after the Revolution they did not have to contend with a time-honored tradition of privileged clergy and church as was true in the Old World. The idea of church as a clerical preserve was not part of the colonial heritage, and the absence of a bishop undercut the tradition of a monarchial rule in the church. For this reason it would be much easier to graft the spirit of democracy onto the church during the period of reorganization.[1]

This they did, imitating their Protestant neighbors in casting aside deference due to aristocracy, wealth, or power. There is no evidence that post-colonial Catholics planned to cast aside old dogmas and religious practices as well, but they expected the priests to act differently, more open-handedly and cooperatively in this new, democratic age. Given the scarcity of priests and their heavy schedules, such expectations might have counted for little were it not for John Carroll, a priest who, due to a series of unusual coincidences, assumed leadership of the American church after the Revolution. His writings indicate his own enthusiasm about the changes that were occurring in this country. While the war was still being waged, he wrote to a friend: "I am glad to inform you that the fullest and largest system of toleration is adopted in almost all the American states; public protection and encouragement are extended alike to all denominations, and Roman Catholics are members of congress, assemblies, and hold military posts, as well as others."[2]

Carroll clearly saw obvious compatibility between his Catholic beliefs and republican principles, like securing the blessings of liberty, establishing justice, and promoting the general welfare. A member of a gentrified Maryland family that had been in America for generations, Carroll had become a Jesuit priest and was living in Europe when the Jesuit order was suppressed by the pope in 1773 (a bizarre situation due to demands from major European monarchs regarding Jesuit financial and missionary misadventures). Somewhat disillusioned about the benefits of monarchy, Carroll returned to America the next year. He and all ex-Jesuits were advised by their former superiors to either join a local diocese or enter a religious order in their area. But there was no diocese in America and no religious order in the area, so Carroll by this odd circumstance became a kind of freelance priest.

By another odd circumstance, he and his cousin Charles Carroll (the only Catholic to sign the Declaration of Independence) were asked to accompany Benjamin Franklin to Canada in 1776 on a mission to urge that country to side with the revolution. The effort was unsuccessful, but John Carroll formed a lasting friendship with Franklin that would prove very useful. When the hostilities ended, Carroll served the Catholic community for the next five years. He observed a definite lack of initiative among the Catholic priests. He wrote to a friend, "The clergymen here continue to live in the old form. It is the effect of habit.... I regret that indolence prevents any form of administration being adopted."[3] With the increasing flow of immigrants from Europe, accompanied by their priests he feared that the American church of the future would be fashioned according to the old model and the thrust toward a new, democratic model would be lost forever. In 1783 he rallied the priests together (most of them ex-Jesuits like himself) at a meeting near Georgetown and presented a plan of action. Together they wrote a constitution for the clergy and assisted Carroll in writing a letter to Pope Pius VI.

He chose to proceed carefully, not extolling the advantages of democracy, but rather stressing the uncertain status of the church in America. He strongly advised the pope against appointing an apostolic delegate (that is, a papal representative to the new country). "You are not ignorant that in these United States our religious system has undergone a revolution, if possible, more extraordinary than our political one," he wrote. "This is a blessing and advantage which it is our duty to preserve and improve with the utmost prudence, by demeaning ourselves on all occasions as subjects zealously attached to our government and avoiding to give any jealousies on account of any dependence on foreign jurisdictions more than that which is essential to our religion." He then urged the pope "to place the episcopal powers, at least such as are most essential, in the hands of one amongst us, whose virtue, knowledge, and integrity of faith, shall be certified by ourselves."[4]

The letter might in all likelihood have been instantly rejected by the pope as an exercise of audacity by this little coterie of unknown priests, since it flew in the face of established precedent. But it so happened that Benjamin Franklin, who was on diplomatic duty at the time in Paris, heard of the unusual request, and it is reported that "he exerted all his influence to press for his good friend's appointment."[5] Franklin's influence prevailed, though not quite as the American priests had hoped. In 1784 the Vatican appointed Carroll as "Vicar Apostolic and Superior of the Mission to the United States." These foreign-sounding titles made him the papal representative in the United States, the very thing Carroll hoped to avoid. But at least it gave him authority to act on behalf of the church, and he used it to further his ideas.

For the rest of the 1780s the blueprint of an inculturated, national church emerged under Carroll's leadership — one committed to democracy and to the Catholic faith. Among its characteristics was endorsement of the separation of church and state as an ideal and not as a temporary concession to political reality. The blueprint included the creation of a school (Georgetown Academy) as a "nursery" for American vocations to the priesthood and later the opening of a theology school (St. Mary's in Baltimore). It encouraged the celebration of Mass and the administration of the sacraments in the English language and insisted that all foreign priests learn to speak English and become sensitized to American culture. It also provided for laity to nominate pastors for their parishes, encouraged the settlement of disputes by parish arbitration committees, and urged friendly relations with Protestant congregations. Perhaps the most enduring aspect of the plan was the spread of the lay trustee system in Catholic parishes.

Trusteeism has often been portrayed in Catholic history as a terrible innovation, even a heresy, because of some of its more spectacular failures. In fact, it proved highly successful in most parishes for years to come and was anything but innovative in its origins. With only a handful of clergy serving them, the original Catholic settlers passed on their experiences and their expectation of full congregational involvement and control. Carroll saw good reason to make it the norm. The system, says historian Dolan, involved a separation between parish temporal and spiritual matters, with elected lay trustees having broad authority in the temporal area:

> They were the parish business managers and their major concern was financial — collection of pew rents, purchasing an organ, selling gravesites in the parish cemetery, determining the salary of the priest, and paying off debts. They also supervised the work of those who worked for the parish such as the organist and the priest. The priest was responsible for the church's spiritual affairs. When the priest and the trustees did not agree on some issue, be it salary or the quality of preaching, then conflict did occur and it could be very bitter and prolonged. But as Patrick Carey, the recognized authority on this issue, noted, such conflict took place in relatively few Catholic parishes. In the vast majority of Catholic parishes...the trustee system worked well, and it remained the people's choice for local church government.[6]

On one point, Carroll was adamant. He sternly opposed the idea that trustees, on their own authority, could fire a priest.

After two years as vicar apostolic, Carroll and his colleagues decided they should again petition for a bishop from their own ranks. In a letter to the head of the Congregation for the Propagation of the Faith, Carroll got right to the point. What is most needed in America, he said, is a bishop with his own authority operating out of a distinct, geographical diocese. Protestant fears are aroused, he argued, when the church's leader is seen as the delegate of the head of a foreign state, and "this fear will increase if they know that an ecclesiastical superior is so appointed as to be removable at the pleasure of the Sacred Congregation for the Propagation of the Faith, or any other tribunal out of the country."[7]

Correspondence continued slowly between Rome and Baltimore until in 1788 the pope said yes, the priests could select their own bishop, and yes, they could decide which city would be the diocesan headquarters. The priests met and elected Carroll as their choice (twenty-four votes for him, four for other candidates, and three abstentions). Finally in 1790, John Carroll traveled to England to be consecrated bishop, since there was no bishop in the United States to perform the ceremony.

The Experiment Disintegrated

We do not know what further progressive strides this thoroughly Catholic, thoroughly American church based in Baltimore might have taken in the remaining fifteen years of Carroll's life, because once he had accepted the bishop's hat and staff, he became suddenly cautious. With that caution, the blueprint drawn up by Carroll began to come apart. Says Dolan, "As striking as its emergence was in the 1780s, the more startling was its disintegration in the 1790s." At the priests' synod in Baltimore in 1791 regulations regarding the Mass and sacraments and the financial support of the clergy were determined, but they appeared to be little more than copies of laws from old European synods. Carroll admitted the absence of any innovations and thought the decrees "too unimportant" to be even worth publishing. The synod did concur that the practice of electing bishops should continue, agreeing with Carroll that "otherwise, we never shall be viewed kindly by our government here, and discontents, even among our own Clergy, will break out."[8]

Indeed, by then it was clear new bishops were needed in the growing areas of Boston, Philadelphia, New York, and Bardstown, Kentucky (near Louisville). However, no elections were held. Instead, Carroll consulted with the "older and more worthy" clergy and then personally submitted his recommendations for bishop to Rome. None of his choices were native-born Americans. He used the same process in selecting a coadjutor bishop for his own Baltimore diocese. As time passed, the idea of electing bishops was dropped and eventually forbidden, as was the practice of having Mass in the English language. In an 1810 synod Carroll and the new bishops ordered the priests under their jurisdiction to "celebrate the whole Mass in the Latin language." Emphasis on other characteristics of the blueprint disappeared. Later when the need arose for more new dioceses and more new bishops, Carroll wrote to the pope, asking him in a most uncharacteristic tone to "instruct us as to how we are to provide in the future [for bishops] and how should the bishops be chosen."[9]

Historians wonder what happened to this charismatic churchman who devoted himself to grafting the spirit of democracy onto Roman Catholicism in the new world. Was it advancing age (he was sixty-five when consecrated bishop)? Was he possibly threatened by the Vatican with penalties if he continued developing the blueprint? Is there perhaps something inherently numbing in the episcopal consecration ceremony itself that renders recipients submissive ever after? (One could cite innumerable historical precedents for such an explanation.)

The more likely answer is that the man who returned to Baltimore in 1790 discovered that circumstances had changed and the ground was moving too quickly beneath his feet. The string of coincidences that promoted a democratic inculturation was now being offset by a new set moving in the opposite direction. First, there is evidence that the fallout from the French Revolution of 1789 frightened him, as it did many Catholic leaders. He spoke out against "anarchy and insurrection" and worried that the new spirit of ecclesiastical democracy might go so far as to force "disunion with the Holy See [that is, the pope]." Second, due to the growing Catholic population, Carroll had to attract foreign priests. And they came in large numbers, many of them French clergy fleeing the excesses of their own revolution. Many of these were horrified to discover that ideas of freedom and independence similar to those that raged in France were germinating inside the very body of American Catholicism. And they were outspoken in their opposition to them, thus causing tensions and quarrels in parishes where the democratic spirit had taken root. Third, though the trustee system was generally successful, the catastrophic, headline-generating cases where it did not work tended to exhaust the energies of its best episcopal supporters.

By way of example, consider the case of St. Mary's parish in Charleston, South Carolina, which strained the patience of Carroll and two bishops who came after him for some twenty years. It involved an Irish-born pastor, Felix Gallagher, a succession of French and Irish priests who came to assist or replace him, a hardheaded group of trustees who tried to start a schism, and the Congregation for the Propagation of the Faith, which badly misunderstood what the arguments were all about. The whole thing was apparently triggered by Gallagher's "fondness for spirits." Carroll asked him to "relinquish pastoral care" and appointed a French priest to the parish. The trustees barred the new priest from their meetings and demanded that all communication between him and them be in writing. After undergoing treatment, Gallagher returned and refused to relinquish his position, the French priest left, and another French priest came. He was rejected by the trustees for his inability "to preach clearly and distinctly in the English language."[10] An Irish assistant priest arrived, joined forces with Gallagher, and the two set themselves and half of the congregation against the French priest and the other half. Suspensions and interdicts by the bishops were ignored. And toward the end, the trustees attempted to have an Irish Franciscan priest consecrated as bishop in the schismatic Old Catholic Church of Holland. By the time the controversy ended. Carroll had died (in 1815, at eighty), his successor had also died, and Baltimore's third bishop was exhausted. The man who finally brought peace was the newly named bishop of the newly created diocese of Charleston in 1820, John England.

Despite his apparent disenchantment, Carroll left a mark on the American church — a certain sense of independence, a flair for innovation, and a resentment of dictates from above — that stayed with the church after his passing and remains today.

The Experiment Revived

In a sense John England of Charleston was his immediate successor in carrying on the legacy. He was an Irishman who adapted to democratic ideas with ease and extraordinary enthusiasm. During his twenty-two years as bishop, he was better known to the larger American public than Carroll had ever been. He was a prolific writer, the publisher-editor of the first weekly diocesan paper in the United States, and a skilled rhetorician who used every opportunity to speak publicly about the compatibility of Catholic and republican ideals, one time giving a two-hour address to the U.S. Congress on the subject. In England's analysis,

> the bishop of each [diocese] holds his place, not as the deputy of the Pope, but as a successor to the Apostles; as the governor of each state holds his place not as the deputy of the President, but as vested with the same power which vests the President with his own authority. And all the states are bound together in one federation of which the President

is the head, so are the dioceses collected into one church, of which the Pope is the head.[11]

England drew up a comprehensive constitution based largely on that of the Church of England. It called for a vestry of elected lay trustees in each parish to oversee temporal matters, including the salaries of pastors and the oversight, hiring, and firing of lay employees. He also inaugurated in his diocese a yearly convention with a house of clergy composed of all the priests and a house of the laity made up of elected delegates from the parishes. Each house met separately and passed its own resolutions, but the resolutions became valid only if a majority of both houses and the bishop agreed on them. This extraordinary exercise in yearly collegiality continued until England's death in 1842.

The bishop also determined that these democratic and collegial initiatives should spread beyond one diocese, so he pressed for the creation of a provincial council of the bishops from all the eastern dioceses. The first was held in 1823 amid considerable publicity, and when the archbishop of Baltimore, the principal diocese, declined to summon a second council, England went to Rome and argued his case before Vatican officials:

> The American people know that in the Catholic Church the power of legislation resides in the Pope and the Bishops; and they would be greatly impressed if they would see the church in America regulated in accordance with laws emanating from a Council of Bishops with the approbation of the Holy Father. The conformity of this mode of procedure ... is so striking that it would easily gain not only their obedience but their attachment. But they will never be reconciled to the practice of the bishops, and oftentimes of the priest alone, giving orders without assigning any reason for the same.[12]

The Vatican concurred, and seven of these provincial councils were held between 1823 and 1849. England pressed on. He believed plenary councils, including all the bishops of the United

States, should meet regularly, since the Catholic population was growing at a rate requiring the creation of two or more dioceses a year. Though England did not live to see it, the first plenary was convened in Baltimore in 1852, and two more were held, in 1866 and 1884. These served to unite hierarchy and preserve at least a touch of that independence that Carroll in his earlier days and England thought so important.

Meanwhile, the trustee system faded from the scene in many dioceses and was roundly condemned in others, as newer bishops and immigrant priests preferred the old monarchical approach. Yet it continued to operate at the local level in large numbers of ethnic parishes throughout the nineteenth century and even into the twentieth. German, Polish, Lithuanian, and Slovak immigrants brought with them a tradition of parish involvement and governance that was, in effect, a variation on the U.S. trustee system. Dolan notes how determined Polish people were to preserve their prerogatives: "They resisted strongly and even accepted excommunication rather than go along with the tradition of clerical control in parish affairs. Such resistance was a fact of life in Polish parishes across the country, and parish battles, complete with street riots, church demonstrations, and appeals to Rome, were commonplace."[13] In 1904 arguments over lay ownership of church property escalated to the level of a major schism in the United States. Angry Poles in Chicago, Pennsylvania, and New York severed relations with the Vatican, forming the Polish National Catholic Church, which still exists today. Resistance lives on, most recently in the refusal of parishioners at a Polish Catholic church in St. Louis to turn over parish assets to the archbishop. The controversy was still alive and heated in 2007.

Such extreme measures have been rare in American Catholicism, especially after Pope Leo XIII in the last decade of the nineteenth century issued two encyclicals sharply criticizing American Catholics for too easily accommodating to modern ideas, for claiming that church and state ought to be separate, for stressing activism, and for praising human progress to the detriment of inner spirituality and humble obedience. He called these tendencies "Americanism," and urged bishops and priests to speak strongly against them. So it happened that for much of the twentieth century obedience to authority became the principal Catholic virtue, the most reliable sign of holiness, and the basic requirement for leadership and promotion in Catholic parishes and schools and in the larger church. That was destined to change in the second half of the twentieth century.

Part II

THE PRESENT

Chapter Seven

The Emergence of the Laity

——— ✝ ———

We have an idea...that the Church is the clergy and that the faithful are only our clients and beneficiaries.... This terrible concept has been built into so many of our structures and habits.... It is a betrayal of the truth.

— YVES CONGAR

ONE OF MY FIRST DUTIES as a newly ordained priest in the late 1950s was to serve as chaplain to three of the five Christian Family Movement (CFM) groups in the parish. I relished the opportunity to share my learning and wisdom with the mostly young and middle-aged couples who made up these groups. I met before the meetings with the group leader, and we discussed the chosen topic. But I quickly discovered that an inviolable principle of CFM was that the priest-chaplain was forbidden to speak during the meetings. I was not allowed to correct errors, settle doubtful issues, or bring straying discussions back into line with an authoritative word from on high. I could comment briefly at the end of the sessions, and I always did. However, by then the hour was late and details about the time and place of the next meeting had to be settled.

The seven or eight couples who formed a group were invariably among the most active people in the parish, yet parish activities usually took second place in discussions. The areas of interest were determined by CFM's central committee, which produced inquiry books, treating a different, heavy topic each year, such as politics, poverty, racism, and culture. The aim, using a see-judge-act format, was to discern how this small gathering might bring their Catholic beliefs and principles to bear on real-world issues. As a movement, CFM had grown from a few Chicago-area groups in the early 1940s to more than a hundred thousand groups worldwide in the 1950s. CFM was never widely endorsed by the hierarchy, though one of the founding couples, Pat and Patty Crowley, were awarded a medal in 1957 by Pope Pius XII. My experience in CFM was among the most profound I had as a priest. No, I didn't get to talk much. Instead, I learned that something really exciting was occurring in the church. Laymen and laywomen were training themselves to critically scrutinize the institutions of society (including the church), to trust their experiences and insights, and to work for change where needed. I had come upon a manifestation of a historic trend: the emergence of the laity.

A Gradual Awakening

After papal infallibility was decreed at Vatican Council I in 1871, a kind of shroud descended over the church. Since we had an infallible pope, many thought, why would we ever need another general council? Why, for that matter, would there be a need for future consultations with bishops, theologians, and, least of all, the laity? Archbishop Henry Edward Manning of England declared, "Dogma has conquered history," by which he meant that objections to papal teaching on any basis were futile, since the papal word was the final word. And British publisher H. G. Ward was looking forward to finding infallible declarations on the front page of his newspaper almost daily. For others, this new church seemed to fit the words of the Grand Inquisitor: "We have corrected Thy work and founded it upon miracle, mystery and authority." For the Catholic laity, it was indeed an era of miracle-oriented piety, utter submission to papal authority, and a church with ready answers to every question.

Still, there was too much ferment in the world for a state of inertia to remain undisturbed. Modern ideas about philosophy, psychology, and the natural sciences were blooming everywhere. It was inevitable that some would take root in the environs of the church; the drive to participate, to have a voice, would not be squelched. In the latter years of the nineteenth century Catholic scholars in France and England began to apply the historical-critical method, already in use by Protestants, to the study of theology. In effect, they were saying that dogma has not conquered history, that there exists a kind of evolution in our understanding of the Bible and in the doctrines of the church. This movement, labeled "Modernism" by Vatican authority, was condemned in 1907 by Pius X, and the oath against its basic thrusts was required of every priest from that time forward; only in 1967 was the oath rescinded.

In the 1930s a plant with hardier roots appeared in France, where the urban working class had largely given up on the church. It was called Catholic Action and had the tentative support of Pope Pius XI, who defined it as "the participation of the laity in the apostolate of the hierarchy." Given the crisis conditions, the church was seeking some assistance from the laity in what was and would remain — at least theoretically — the hierarchy's business. Not surprisingly, the movement stalled until a Belgian priest, Canon Joseph Cardijn, borrowed from the communists a technique they had been using with success. He formed small cells of Belgian factory workers and persuaded them to meet regularly and report on their working conditions. He then urged them to judge what they were seeing in the light of gospel principles and eventually to develop action plans on the basis of their judgments. Using this see-judge-act approach, these Young Christian Worker (YCW) groups grew quickly and spread to France, Holland, and Germany. The members were becoming at one and the same time social activists in their work environments and enthusiasts for the Christian message. The YCW movement crossed the ocean to America after World War I where it caught on in large industrial areas and seeded two spin-offs, the Young Christian Students and the Christian Family Movement. The movements dissipated in the social upheaval of the 1960s but not before educating and inspiring a whole generation of Americans with a different idea of what it means to be a lay Catholic.

Meanwhile in France, scholars were developing a theology of the laity that would complement what was occurring at the action level. They included Dominicans Marie-Dominique Chenu and Yves Congar and Jesuits Jean Daniélou and Henri de Lubac. Of these, Congar, a historical theologian, contributed perhaps the most in his book *Lay People in the Catholic Church,* published in 1953. Because of his overt criticism of the church, his support of ecumenism, and his radical views on the role of the laity, Congar was in almost constant trouble with his superiors from 1939 until 1958 (when John XXIII was elected pope). His books were repeatedly under fire or banned, and he was exiled from France for long periods on three different occasions.

Paul Lakeland in his book *The Liberation of the Laity* explores at length some of Congar's themes, which seemed revolutionary in their day, though much less so today.

Consent: Although he accepts the hierarchical structure of the church as a given, Congar finds the texts of early Christianity as "absolutely communitarian." For him there must be a balance, "a meeting and harmonizing between a hierarchical communication from above and a community's consent."

Independence: Congar sees the contributions of the layperson as distinct from that of the priest and the monk. There is one source of the church, he says, "but it flows in two ways — from the apostolic ministry and the sacraments and also through the personal life of the laity who have received God's gifts." In this way "divine grace builds the church from below."

Priesthood: While the ordained priest has special responsibilities not shared with the laity pertaining to the celebration of the sacraments, especially Penance and Eucharist, "all other aspects of the priesthood are shared by clergy and laity." The laity's priesthood is a "true priesthood," not a watered-down derivative, in Congar's theology.

Service: The job of the priests is not to make the laity the long arm of the clergy, telling them what they've got to do, "but to make them believing men and women, adult Christians, leaving them to meet and fulfill the concrete demands of their Christianity." This means "engaging the world and taking responsibility for it through humble service."

Secularity: Congar insists on recognizing that the secular world is important and valuable in its own right. And he rejects the world-hating tendencies of those spiritualities that relativize earthly life in comparison to the spiritual realities of the life to come.

In all these areas Congar was departing from the time-honored definition of the church of Robert Bellarmine: "The community brought together by the profession of the same Christian faith and conjoined in the communion of the same sacraments, under the government of the legitimate pastors and especially the one vicar of Christ on earth, the Roman Pontiff."[1]

Co-equals in Christ

In Vatican II's Dogmatic Constitution on the Church (*Lumen Gentium*) and in the Vatican Decree on the Apostolate of the Laity, Congar's ideas became the official positions of the Catholic Church. Some examples:

For their part, the faithful join in the offering of the Eucharist by virtue of their royal priesthood. Taking part in the Eucharistic sacrifice . . . they offer the Divine Victim to God and offer themselves along with it.[2]

Allotting his gifts to everyone according to His will, He [the Holy Spirit] distributes special graces among the faithful of every rank. By these He makes them fit and ready to undertake the various tasks and offices ... for the renewal and upbuilding of the Church.[3]

Now the laity are called in a special way to make the Church present and operative in those places and circumstances where only through them can she become the salt of the earth.[4]

Christ the great Prophet ... continually fulfills His prophetic office until His full glory is revealed. He does this not only through the hierarchy who teach in His name ... but also through the laity.[5]

An individual layman, by reason of his knowledge, competence or outstanding ability ... is permitted to and sometimes even obliged to express his opinion on things which concern the good of the Church.... Let the sacred pastors recognize and promote the dignity as well as the responsibility of the layman in the Church. Let them willingly make use of his prudent advice.... Further, let them encourage the layman so that he may undertake tasks on his own initiative.[6]

The laity must take on the renewal of the temporal order as their own special obligation. Led by the light of the gospel and the mind of the church ... let them act directly and definitively in the temporal sphere.[7]

But the laity too share in the priestly, prophetic and royal office of Christ and therefore have their own role to play in the mission of the whole People of God.... Incorporated ... through baptism ... they are assigned to the apostolate by the Lord himself.[8]

If not for the timely intervention of Archbishop Leo-Joseph Suenens of Belgium during the preparation for Vatican II, the fingerprints of Congar and his theological colleagues would not be found on these documents or others voted on by the council. Convinced that Pope John XXIII's *aggiornamento* would be stillborn if the conservative and fearful Roman curia prepared all the discussion papers for the council, he persuaded the pope to let him put some "order" in the material. He called on Congar and others to help shape the texts. When everything came before the assembled bishops, concessions had to be made so that the curia and their associates in the hierarchy would not be entirely turned off. The result after debate was a somewhat schizophrenic combination of top-down and bottom-up theology throughout the council's documents. This is one reason why defenders of nineteenth-century theology can find Bellarmine-like authoritarian emphasis in certain sections, while *aggiornamento* advocates point to the new thrust totally at odds with the old way.

Suenens remained confident that in the end this new role of the laity would make all the difference. In *Coresponsibility in the Church,* a book he authored three years after the council, Suenens wrote about the effects of collegiality and democracy in church affairs. An "undeniable process of osmosis and imitation between the manner of ruling in the secular world and in the church" is inevitable, he says, and Vatican II was "notable by reason of its move in the direction of democratization." This did not mean for him that a simple vote by the majority should decide every issue. Rather, he conceived of the church as a tripartite arrangement of monarchy, oligarchy, and democracy — the very system proposed by the decretists and scholars of the twelfth century and raised again during the three-pope chaos in the fifteenth century. The papacy supplies the monarchic element, in Suenens's analysis; the bishops of the world represent the oligarchic; and the faithful, the People of God, constitute the democratic element. There is every reason, he says, why the full church should have a voice in at least the governance of the church, and a healthy discussion on this "will certainly influence the status of the laity in the church of tomorrow."[9]

In his remaining years Suenens urged Pope Paul VI to initiate the new age by decentralizing the papacy. Suenens saw it as unworkable in an ever more complex world. However blessed and talented, he was convinced that one man could not function with executive, legislative, and judicial power over an organization in his hands — as if, in American terms, the president was at the same time the speaker of the house, the majority leader of the Senate, and the chief justice of the Supreme Court — with veto power over all these institutions. Suenens viewed the church's laity moving in the direction of coresponsibility, not waiting for permission but pressing for change, even demanding it. Toward the end of his book, Suenens writes,

> Today one thing is certain: the era of absolute monarchy must be exercised within a new sociological context.... The leader is no longer the man who has all the answers but the man who succeeds in creating the environment in which dialogue, research, and constructive criticism are possible by the gradual process of consent. I think this is the future direction of the Church — all parts moving together through, with, and under authority.[10]

For this to happen, says Lakeland,

> it will be necessary for the laity to take charge of their own liberation. It cannot be the work of bishops or priests, though they can certainly assist. The primary way they can assist is by stepping aside. If the laity have been marginalized in the church of the past, and they surely have, then they must claim the center of the stage for a time. Those who have occupied that center stage can stand aside willingly or be pushed aside. That is up to them.[11]

Progress and Backlash

That the council had an impact on lay Catholics is undeniable. By placing such heavy emphasis on baptism as the sacrament that incorporates all into the Body of Christ, it dealt a body blow to the class consciousness that had been a hallmark of the church for centuries. The hallmark is giving way, though begrudgingly. Theologian Ladislas Orsy notes how Holy Orders, the sacrament of priesthood, had acquired a disproportionate and "overabundant symbolism in clothing, titles and speech," while there was nothing similar in connection with baptism. Even now, says Orsy, canon law still speaks of the "sacred pastors" but never of the "sacred laity."[12]

When I was sitting (silently) at Christian Family Movement meetings in the 1950s, there were hints of what was to come. Their immersion in the movement gave a boost to their spirituality and made them — me too — almost giddy about the possibilities of a servant church in the modern world, about working together for peace and reconciliation among races and nations. And they had some ideas too about the governance of the church, especially since many of these CFMers were fully aware of the social encyclicals of the popes and the liturgical movement. But beyond these stimulating meetings and the activities they inspired, nothing had changed. Sunday Mass was as it always had been for the previous four hundred years, a priestly preserve in a priestly language with minimal or no participation from the pews. The faithful went to communion, receiving the host on their tongues, provided they had fasted from midnight and did not have any unforgiven mortal sins on their souls. And judging by the long lines outside the confessionals on Saturday, mortal sin was a common occurrence in those days. Decisions about what activities would or would not happen in the parish were always made by "Monsignor," a man who radiated charm and steely authority. This was his parish, his church, his school, and everybody knew it — especially those annoying CFM folks who were always coming up with ideas about inviting in radical speakers.

Now, some fifty years later, it's all different. Or is it? Laypersons read the Scriptures from the pulpit every Sunday, place the Eucharist in the hands of their neighbors and offer them the cup of consecrated wine. The people sing hymns, participate in the Mass prayers, shake hands with those around them at the appropriate time, and sometimes seem deeply touched by their experience of liturgy. The laity serve on parish councils and parish finance committees, organize and teach in parish education programs, and prepare converts for entrance into the church. As never before laity in many parishes work as salaried pastoral associates, directors of religious education, directors of liturgy, and parish business managers.

In 2006 there were more than 31,000 paid lay ministers in U.S. parishes. The U.S. Bishops Conference called them "Co-Workers in the Vineyard of the Lord" in an upbeat 2005 pastoral statement. There were another 18,000 in professional training for lay ministry, about six times the number of U.S. seminarians. Soon, said the National Pastoral Life Center, there will be more professional lay ministers than priests serving in parishes, especially since the number of active priests is dwindling, while the average age of priests is rising. A 2003 study reported more priests over the age of ninety than under thirty. In 1950 the United States averaged one priest for every 650 Catholics; by 2005 it was one priest for every 2,200 Catholics. Although the permanent deacons are technically clerics, they are more closely akin to laity, and the American church had some 15,000 deacons functioning in 2005. In short, the emergence of the laity has turned into a virtual explosion, and providentially so, it seems. If not for that surge in lay power, the Catholic Church would be barely functioning.

Meanwhile, six important professional church organizations banded together to assist this growing pool of laity, as well as the ranks of overworked and aging clergy, in dealing with the new situation. The Emerging Models of Pastoral Excellence Project is a collaboration of groups including the National Association of Lay Ministers, the National Association of Church Personnel Administrators, and the National Federation of Priest Councils. Funded by the Lilly Foundation, the project aims to develop collaborative and competent leadership in this lay-emerging era. Besides gathering data and disseminating information, concentrations include identifying and forming lay leaders, developing ways to make parish councils work effectively, encouraging theological reflection, and piloting new models of shared ministry.

Unfortunately, the increase in lay involvement has not been matched with any officially endorsed increase of the lay voice in decision making. By virtue of canon law and papal preference, Monsignor is still in charge. This is not to deny that some pastors do function as if the parish operation were a democracy. They are leaders who respect the wisdom and leadership capabilities of their people (usually because they have modeled those characteristics within the parish). When it's time to vote, such pastors cast one vote like everybody else, and they abide by the results. But clergy and laity are well aware that when such a pastor retires or is transferred, there is no guarantee the church-from-below style of operation will survive. The chances are (and they are growing) that the new, younger, and fresher pastor will introduce a decidedly top-down style of administration. This tends to happen because Pope John Paul II encouraged a restoration movement to curb alleged excesses of the Vatican II reform and to resurrect much of the leadership and devotional styles of the pre–Vatican II era.

Many hoped the 1983 revision of the Code of Canon Law would reflect the new regard for the role of laity expressed in the council. It did not; instead, it eyed spreading developments such as parish councils with extreme suspicion. Parish councils have "a consultative vote only," reminded the code, and are permitted to exist only if a bishop judges them "to be opportune" after "consulting with his priests."[13]

In 1987, some twenty years after the council, a synod of bishops was held in Rome on the status of the laity. In preparation for the event the American bishops oversaw a consultative process, which included input from some 200,000 people. However, when the 230 invited bishops — along with 60 lay *auditores* (listeners) — gathered, they heard the pope's grave concern about the extent of lay empowerment. He did not like the term "ministry" used in any lay church activity, and he expressed fear that the church was heading toward a "clericalization of the laity and a laicization of the clergy." Any theology that does not clearly note the difference "in essence" between the priesthood of the clergy and the priesthood of the laity is seriously flawed, he said, and must be corrected. The bishops were forbidden to share with the press the text of their prepared statements or to make public their conclusions. As it happened some of the material did leak out, indicating that the bishops, while generally satisfied with the process of empowerment, were more concerned about the role of women and the importance of the local church. Nevertheless, the main topic of discussion at the council was how the local church should relate to the new lay movements, such as Opus Dei and Communion and Liberation, much favored by John Paul.

His determination to boost the image of the clerical priesthood surfaced again in the 1997 Vatican "Instruction Regarding the Collaboration of the Non-ordained Faithful in the Sacred Ministry of Priests" (whose title alone reveals the tone of the document). The non-ordained person may never be allowed to use titles such as "pastor," "chaplain," "coordinator," or "moderator," said the instruction, since that would confuse their role with that of a priest. Nor may a layperson ever be allowed to preach or give the homily at Mass; nor may such a person ever preside at a liturgy or wear a stole or other kind of vestment. Extraordinary ministers of communion should be used only in cases of necessity, said the instruction, lest the practice become habitual. Once again, it was made clear that parish councils and parish finance councils are advisory bodies only and their decisions invalid unless approved by the pastor.[14]

Whatever morale benefits these actions provided the clergy, they sent a contrary, reactionary message to the laity. It is not difficult to detect a sense of disappointment, even cynicism, among the members of many parishes, and this is particularly so among those laity who took very seriously their new role in the church. In a 2005 survey by the National Pastoral Life Center, lay ministers across the country listed "interactions with the clergy" as the second aspect of their work most in need of improvement. "Salary" was the first area listed, though average salaries in most lay ministries have doubled, even tripled, since 1990. More than a third of the ministers said they had "often" or "sometimes" considered leaving their job during the past year. Among the reasons listed were "conflict with pastors" and "burnout." If paid ministers are losing heart, it's certain that volunteer ministers in the parish are also getting singed.

According to Catholic author Alice Camille, "What frustrates folks in the pew is that even in the third millennium of the church, most of the terms of their membership and role are dictated to them as though they were children. And when they reach out to accept greater responsibility and assume more leadership, in keeping with virtually every other aspect of their adult lives, they are abruptly 'put in their place.' "[15]

Camille's point about "every other aspect of their lives" is a salient one. Adults in the business, corporate, or academic worlds today expect to be treated as such; they hope to be respected, to have a sense of partnership with co-workers and superiors, to have a voice in decisions, or at least to be informed about the reasons behind decisions of upper management. When these elements are absent from their jobs, dissatisfaction and resentment develop.

Then came the priest abuse scandal of 2002. It revealed, as nothing had before, how little input laity have in the decision-making processes of their church. Their children were the victims of abuse, yet such was the nature of the clerical system that they were never consulted or informed about what had been going on for years until the press broke the story. A widespread culture of secrecy had hidden the truth for years. The lay reaction was fiery and bitter. Catholics began looking at the church as an institution in ways they had never done before.

A Different Kind of Laity

I don't think the abuse scandal of itself will be enough to trigger the kind of change that is needed. It's a fact that large numbers of the laity still prefer their traditional stance of passivity. Much depends then on the courage, skill, and persistence of those laymen and laywomen who are sensitive to the signs of the times, studying them in relation to the movement of history. Church reform, as we have seen, has been the perennial subject of lay concern, yet never before have the laity been so well equipped to take the initiative.

First, by placing such weighty emphasis on baptism as the quintessential sacrament, which incorporates us all into the Body of Christ and makes us sharers in his role as priest, king, and prophet, Vatican II dealt a mighty blow to centuries-old distinctions of class and clan. Less and less are Catholics cowed by the claims of naked authority. They know who they are and expect to work collaboratively and equally with other church members of whatever rank or condition. Gradually, they are redefining what it means to be an adult Catholic.

Second, the theological foundation is in place. The Vatican II doctrine on the dignity, rights, and obligations of the laity is neither fad nor opinion. It will not go away and cannot be buried, regardless of the position of one or more Vatican pontificates. It is the teaching of the Roman Catholic Church as set forth in a valid general council. Moreover, the theology has since been growing and developing within the theological community and through books, conferences, college courses, and the experience of the laity. The teaching will not be reversed nor treated as inconsequential for long.

Third, there exists in much of the Western world today a different kind of Catholic laity than the institutional church has ever had to deal with before in its two-millennium history. It is a laity that is better educated, not just in secular matters but in history and theology; better able to communicate views and opinions widely and instantly, thanks to modern technology; and better able to articulate its concerns in a reasoned, credible manner. It is a laity many of whose members have an education in ecclesiastical matters equal or superior to that of their pastors or bishops.

Fourth, the laity in substantial numbers are already in the places of influence, if not in the positions of influence. As paid employees they are in the rectories, churches, diocesan offices, Catholic universities, schools of theology, even seminaries. They are not names on a petition but faces with eyes and ears more sensitive now than ever to the follies and foibles of leadership. Consider the great coming forth of the laity at the Council of Constance some six hundred years ago. I believe it arose from the same impulse to seek voice and involvement that has been stirring in the modern church since Vatican II. The faithful arrived at Constance by donkey cart, on horseback, or on foot to demand reform (discussed in chapter 5). But they were on the whole illiterate, unschooled in theological distinctions, incapable of organizing on a broad scale. Their sheer presence was their only weapon. Though it served their purpose for the moment, it could not become a permanent, demanding presence. The church soon fell back onto hard times. That is not the case today. The laity have access and opportunity to present a sustained visible presence, as illustrated, for example, by the Call to Action organization and, very dramatically, by the impact of the Voice of the Faithful movement.

Fifth, many laypersons have already experienced a taste of democratization through their active membership on parish or diocesan councils whose leaders take seriously the lay role. Others are serving as pastoral administrators in parishes without resident priest-pastors and gaining experience in collaborative leadership. They see firsthand how decisions reached by an open, shared process work better than those settled by an edict from above or later overturned without explanation. They will never be content to give their time to bodies that lack decision-making authority or that may be disbanded should a bishop decide their existence "not opportune."

Chapter Eight

Learning to Live with Democracy

———— ✝ ————

If authoritarian methods alienate and dispirit workers in corporations, they will alienate and dispirit members of the Church; if participatory methods empower and motivate workers...the same will be true of the Church.

— TERENCE NICHOLS

O NE YEAR AFTER the priest abuse story exploded all over America in 2002, the Yale University Catholic Center sponsored a conference entitled "Governance, Accountability, and the Future of the Catholic Church." To set the tone, Donald Wuerl, then bishop of Pittsburgh, gave the keynote address and journalist Peter Steinfels offered a response. I think the interchange between the two illustrates the static state of the church's institutional leadership and the moves it must eventually make in order to survive.

"We do not vote or take a headcount to determine what we should believe or how the church should be structured," says Wuerl.

When we address accountability in the church, we must be careful not to use a political model for a reality that transcends human political institutions.... At every level in the church we are accountable to the Gospel, to the teaching of the church on faith and morals, and to the liturgical and canon law that directs and gives order to the mission and

115

ministry of the church. No one can claim — either by word
or deed — to stand above or outside the structure of the
faith and order that is essential to the church.[1]

Wuerl's words echoed the response of other bishops and clerics when the scandal broke: Yes, we will handle the problem, but
let no one dare to tamper with the changeless structure of the
church as we define it. Steinfels replies:

> There is something more than a little disconcerting about
> the swift move from Jesus' constitution of the church to its
> contemporary manifestation, complete with references in a
> single sentence to the gospel, magisterial teaching on faith
> and morals, and canon law, followed in the next sentence
> by a reference to the "structure of the faith and order that
> is essential to the church." I know that Bishop Wuerl is
> as aware as I am of the two-thousand-year history of strik-
> ingly different ways in which the faith has been understood
> and lived and to the even more strikingly different forms its
> essential structure and order have taken. This is a history
> that alerts us to both unhappy deviations and legitimate
> variety. If nothing else, this history warns us against privi-
> leging our own moment as the perfect realization of Jesus'
> intentions and the Holy Spirit's guidance.

Steinfels also takes issue with

> the sharp distinctions in Bishop Wuerl's presentation be-
> tween making use of political models, by which he seems
> to mean *democratic* models, and fidelity to a founding
> truth. "We do not as Catholics vote on the articles of the
> Creed," he reminds us. But once upon a time, I believe,
> some bishops did — at a council called and in important
> ways controlled by an emperor. "We do not vote or take
> a headcount on what we should believe or how the church
> should be structured," Bishop Wuerl states, and yet he cites
> authoritative documents on the structure of the church that
> were indeed legitimated by a headcount. I think headcounts

have played an important role in the Holy Spirit's guidance of the church.

This transcendent church, notes Steinfels, reflects a wide variety of political models it has absorbed over the centuries: "Catholic institutions and governance incorporate elements of imperial Rome, medieval feudalism and monarchy, Renaissance bureaucracy, modern diplomacy, and the nineteenth-century nation state."

Democracy as Demon

There is a longstanding policy among Catholic apologists like Bishop Wuerl to lay a mantle of changelessness over everything associated with the church, from its essential structure, to the use of the Latin language, to the shape of communion wafers. Creeping changelessness has been an instrument, I believe, to stifle that ageless thrust toward voice and participation in the church. Yet, as Steinfels notes, the truth is that the church has accommodated itself to, and integrated into its own operations, a host of worldly political models like imperial rule and monarchy. Unfortunately, the church today still reflects elements of medieval feudalism, a political system based on top-down control and strict, bottom-up obedience and loyalty. And critics have been quick to point out that this is a major reason why the abuse of children by priests continued as long as it did without correction or public awareness.

It is interesting that Steinfels would mention the fact that important decisions in the church were once made by headcount. It is easy to forget that, because this is not our usual custom anymore. And that brings us into the intimidating presence of the large elephant in Catholicism's living room. According to the church's canon law, only clerics are empowered to make decisions, and they do so in a decidedly hierarchical way. The pope exercises supreme power. When he calls a synod of bishops, their conclusions are all advisory; they may be accepted, rejected, or ignored by the pope. Likewise in a diocese the bishop is in charge, and all his advisers and councils of priests or laypersons are for consultative purposes only. In the parish the pastor rules; the parish council or financial council may propose but he disposes. The elephant is the main reason many people will scoff at the very idea of democracy and Catholicism appearing in the same sentence. But democracy is a many-layered thing. As an idea it has shown a peculiar congruity with that perennial pressure from below discussed in earlier chapters.

The Enlightenment in the seventeenth and the eighteenth centuries marked a turning point in European history. It championed ideals like the universal rights of humankind, the importance of secular values, the potential of unfettered human reason, and the need for representative governments. It was creating the modern world. Every step of the way the church saw only threats to religious belief. Many early founders of the Enlightenment were not anti-religion; they were "deists" who acknowledged a creator God. But this was a God who left the world to its own devices, who, like a great clockmaker, wound up his cosmic creation, set it on a table and left the premises, letting it tick on until it stopped. Needless to say, they had little interest in prayer, miracles, or other dealings between this world and the other side, since no one was listening. To whatever extent the spirit of the Grand Inquisitor was operative in the hierarchy, the new thinking appeared to it as certain shipwreck for the institution.

If modernity stressed reason, the church stressed faith. If modernity stressed human progress, the church stressed original sin. If modernity stressed freedom of thought, the church stressed the binding nature of its dogmas. If modernity stressed democracy, the church stressed authority. This stress-filled stalemate was to perdure for the better part of four hundred years. If there had been even a small opening for discussion and dialogue between these two rivals, I think the church might well have served as a helpful brake on the runaway exuberance of modernity that led to riots, wars, and mass executions, of which the French Revolution is one well-known example. By the same token, some discussion and dialogue between the two sides might have helped the church realize that many Enlightenment insights were not fundamentally different from some of its own foundational values.

What particularly alarmed church leaders was the claim of secular humanists that reason alone, untouched by faith, would usher in a new era of unlimited progress. And indeed, the spiral of new inventions and new discoveries from the sixteenth century on seemed to justify such claims. In response, the church placed great emphasis on the flawed nature of the material, fallen, secular world. The dominant theme of spirituality reflected the world-denying approach of the Thomas à Kempis classic, *The Imitation of Christ:* "The more I go out among men, the less I come back a man." Better to meditate on higher things than to get mired down in a world destined to perish. Better to spurn the present life in favor of the one to come. The burden of original sin meant that all merely human inventions and institutions (those founded on democratic principles, for example) were neither trustworthy nor durable; they were products of a pride-filled grace-less world and could contribute nothing toward salvation. This attitude of suspicion, even hatred, toward the world penetrated deeply into the Catholic psyche and is still at the center of piety for some members of the church.

However, with the passage of time some Catholic leaders began to realize this dark defense was a distorted exaggeration of the Christian message. John Carroll, the first American bishop, saw no incompatibility between a democratic government and Catholic belief. Nor did he and other early American Catholics in the eighteenth century hesitate to introduce democratic procedures into the governance of the church itself.

Fifty years later in France, Felicité de Lamennais, an activist priest, and several colleagues attracted attention when they publicly declared it was time for the church to be in the forefront of a détente with modernity. Holding out for a return of the old monarchies that supported Catholicism was foolish, he argued. Instead, he said, the church should abandon its gloomy outlook and welcome democratic government, the separation of church and state, freedom of the press, and universal suffrage (even for women). By 1831 de Lamennais had attracted so much support that he went to Rome to present his ideas personally to the pope. Though he waited there for six months, he did not obtain an audience, but rather only an encyclical condemning every one of his ideas. Clearly, the church was not yet ready for this man, who is considered the father of Catholic liberalism. It was not ready thirty-three years later either, in 1864, when Pope Pius IX published his *Syllabus of Errors*. In its summary conclusion it stated that "the Roman Pontiff cannot and ought not to reconcile himself and come to terms with progress, liberalism and modern civilization."[2]

The Rehabilitation of an Idea

But theologians and spiritual writers made more progress when they began to reexamine this deep-seated, world-renouncing spirit among Catholics. Their argument was difficult to refute: The Word, the Second Person of the Blessed Trinity, entered the world and became human because God loved the world. Jesus lived fully in the world, recognizing its proclivity for sin and error, but more importantly, embracing the world even to his own suffering and death — and lifting up and redeeming this world. There is nothing terribly radical in this world-affirming emphasis. In the thirteenth century Thomas Aquinas, following the insights of Aristotle, taught that the things of this world have a value in themselves, as sparks of the divine light; they should not be regarded as inferior realities or mere symbols of what lies in the greater, spiritual world. In so doing, he was preparing — at quite a distance in time — for the birth of the Enlightenment and the birth of modern science. This view of Christianity, so much friendlier to new ideas, suggests that the believer is called on to embrace the world, despite its defects, and to work in cooperation with others who are sincerely involved in the humanization of that world — whether they believe in our God or no God. It is also a view that recognizes that the Holy Spirit is not a prisoner of the church but is working in mysterious, sometimes wonderful ways in the secular world as well.

Writer Paul Lakeland explains this approach, which recognizes the worth, even the holiness, of secularity:

> The person of faith lives in and deals daily with a secular reality that is in no way different from that of the nonbeliever. The world we encounter is exactly the same. The courses of action we take in the world, the priorities we set and the plans we make may be indistinguishable from those of at least the more thoughtful of our agnostic or atheistic fellow citizens. Nor do we have a secret plan or are we possessed of privileged information, so that we live in the world like secret agents.... In the end, our difference is in the story we tell about the world, one that stresses that we are affirmed by God and that we in turn affirm the goodness of the human and natural world.[3]

The church's first practical accommodation to political democracy came toward the end of the nineteenth century. It came late and, like other great turnarounds in church history, it came abruptly and without apology. Because of modernity, the world had experienced a huge growth in population, a tremendous increase in literacy, the birth of popular culture, improvements in transportation and communication — and the arrival of mass production. This last development proved to be an ambiguous one. With it came widespread oppression of workers in Europe and America and calls for deliverance. Pope Leo XIII took a bold step. His 1891 encyclical, *Rerum Novarum* (Concerning New Things), ended the long retreat from the new age, at least to some extent. It urged Catholics to wade in on the side of social justice and reform of the social order. This meant approval of a range of democratic techniques that his predecessor, Pius IX, would have railed against: the organizing of labor unions, freedom of religion and the press, and the creation of democratic constitutions.

According to historian Thomas Bokenkotter, "The encyclical *Rerum Novarum* has been rightly called the *Magna Carta* of social Catholicism, since it summarized the best Catholic thought on the social question, brought the main issues into focus, and laid down the main lines that Catholic social thought would henceforth follow."[4]

Christian-inspired, democratically structured labor unions grew at a phenomenal rate, despite opposition from management and their own internal struggles. They succeeded in bringing a measure of justice and balance to the work world. In Europe after the Second World War, the trade union movement morphed into Christian Democrat political parties, which became the most powerful force in Western Europe and which remain vigorous today. This elevation of the secular would be implicitly endorsed as church teaching in 1963 in the Second Vatican Council's Pastoral Constitution on the Church in the Modern World. It opened with the words: "The joys and hopes, the griefs and anxieties of the men of this age, especially those who are poor or in any way afflicted, these too are the joys and hopes, the griefs and anxieties of the followers of Christ. Indeed, nothing genuinely human fails to raise an echo in their hearts."[5] It also served to disperse the world-opposing gloom of earlier Vatican documents, noting for example that the church "receives a variety of helps from men of every rank and condition. For whoever promotes the human community at the family level, culturally, in its economic, social and political dimensions, such a one... is contributing greatly to the Church community as well."[6]

It was Pope Pius XII who suggested that, all things considered, the best form of civil government just might be democracy. His speeches during World War II vigorously criticized dictatorships such as that found in Nazi Germany, and he went several steps further, finding other forms of government less desirable than democracy, since it appeared as the best suited to create social justice. Perhaps the most dramatic instance of church-supported democracy occurred during Pope John Paul II's long reign. His ringing endorsement of the democratic Solidarity movement in Poland versus the totalitarian Communist government played a significant role in the collapse of the Soviet Union in 1989. The pope never said he supported democracy as a general rule, but he certainly put his stamp and the stamp of the Catholic Church on one of the most successful democratic initiatives of history.

Democracy as Partner

Of course, it is one thing for the church to back political or other civil democracies. It is another to welcome democratization into the inner workings of the church itself. Yet that is a direction in which the church is moving, though not without objection. The first and most obvious objection is a blunt dismissal: "The Catholic Church is not a democracy!" I have heard it from the lips of bishops and laity. It is supposed to settle all arguments, calm all fears. Yet I'm often unsure what the speaker means.

The church does not function like a democracy now? Yes, of course.

The church never functioned like a democracy? I think the record shows that innumerable times it tried and sometimes it really did act democratically for periods of time in the course of history.

The church never will operate like a democracy and never should? This final, absolute declaration alarms me. It echoes what Bishop Wuerl said about the changeless "structure of the faith" and what Peter Steinfels responded about the danger of "privileging our own moment as the perfect realization of Jesus' intentions and the Holy Spirit's guidance."

I know very well that some Catholics prefer a monarchical, top-down form of church governance. It is clean and efficient and requires at bottom only faith and obedience. I know of a Catholic radio preacher who tells his audience they do not have to think deeply about, much less question, the mysteries of the faith because the teaching authority of the church, "the magisterium," takes care of that for you.

Some years ago I spent three days at the Franciscan University of Steubenville, an extremely conservative Catholic institution, researching a story for the *National Catholic Reporter.* When I asked students why they attended this school, I got a wide swath of answers. I remember one young woman in particular who said she was there because "I've done it all and I don't want to live that way anymore." She had become a flight attendant right out of college, she said, and soon got pulled into a routine of sex, alcohol, and drugs. "I need control," she told me. "I need absolute answers, and I find them here." We were sitting in a room with a picture of John Paul II on one wall and Padre Pio on another. She had obviously found stability and refuge in a stormy world. The last thing she needed at that time in her life was a messy democratic church wrestling with different points of view and new ways of approaching old problems. But Catholics have to be careful about mistaking certainty for truth. In the long run, I believe, we get closer to truth by struggling with differing points of view and discovering new ways to approach the perennial problems.

Will the Catholic Church become a democracy? Not in the sense of a secular, "direct" democracy like the one in Switzerland, where citizens are called to the polls numerous times a year to vote on long lists of bills and referendums. And I don't think it will come in the sense of the democracy we have in the United States, where elected representatives in federal, state, and local legislatures vote on behalf of their constituents. Democracy in the church will always be different because it's not just another secular organization. It is, we believe, a divinely founded institution, and it has a hierarchy that is not going to go away. Still, the U.S. hierarchy gave a fleeting glimpse of democracy in its process of creating pastoral letters on nuclear war and the economy in the 1980s.

The greatest obstacle to a full Catholic democracy at this point in history is the church's canon law, which asserts that only popes, bishops, and priests, all male, may hold the positions that determine governance and authentic teaching. Too often "the ordinary faithful are treated less as participants by full right, than as 'valued customers,' of a multi-national producer and retailer of consumer goods," says canon lawyer John Beal. "While the church would have little reason to exist without these 'customers,' they have no essential role to play in the institution's internal decision-making process."[7] The realization of this hard reality had a traumatic effect on many well-intentioned members of Voice of the Faithful in 2002 and ever since. Their suggestion that certain ecclesial structures need reform was not taken in good grace. Some bishops even banned VOTF from church property. James Muller, VOTF founding president, said the imbalance of power resulting from canonical restrictions is actually what made the abuse scandal possible: "With the laity involved in the decision making of the church — with mothers and fathers playing an active role — the sex abuse scandal would never have happened," he declared.[8]

Nevertheless, there are many reasons why some forms of authentic democracy can operate in such a church even now and why fuller forms will come in the future. In a fascinating book, *That All May Be One: Hierarchy and Participation in the Church*, theologian Terence C. Nichols sketches the blueprint of a church that preserves the essence of the old and is open to the new.

If the purpose of the Catholic Church is to build up the Body of Christ and extend the reign of God in the world, he asserts, then its current monarchical structure is not serving that purpose well. Monarchy had its successes, Nichols says, but also its striking deficiencies: "It led to ruptures in the Body, to clericalism, legalism, and in many cases to nominal, merely external observance. Essentially, the Church was unified as much by authoritarian hierarchy as by the Spirit. But the foundations for this authoritarianism were traditions which could not stand critical and historical scrutiny."[9] His critique echoes the view of Cardinal Suenens, who declared soon after Vatican II, "Today one thing is certain: the era of absolute monarchy is over, and authority must be exercised within a new sociological context."

Modern political history, Nichols says, reveals that monarchic rule simply doesn't work for a society that values participation and unity: "All modern Western polities have rejected absolute monarchy as a viable political mode and have embraced some social system of representative government and division of powers in the government as a way of guarding against tyranny. Those countries which have not adopted such checks and balances...have experienced vicious tyrannies." Nichols anticipates the response of those who reject the use of any analogy based on civil government when speaking of the church. The church is indeed different, he acknowledges; it has a divine aspect that grounds its hierarchy:

> But it is also a human organization, and is subject to the same social dynamics as other large organizations. If authoritarian methods alienate and dispirit workers in corporations, they will alienate and dispirit members of the Church; if participatory methods empower and motivate workers, and result in worker identification with organizational goals, the same will be true of the Church.[10]

He cites the considerable weight of studies concerning employer-employee participation. According to experts Benjamin Tregoe and Peter Tobias, "The old command-and-control model that once was the organizing principle of our military and industrial orders has gone the way of the three-martini lunch. The new paradigm emphasizes decentralization, flexibility, and influence more than power, and participation more than one-man or elite rule." In this arrangement, worker teams are given responsibility for ordering supplies, setting schedules, even electing their supervisors and hiring new members of their team. Such a system works, of course, only if the leadership is well-trained, sensitive and empowering.[11]

According to management specialist Rensis Linkert, "Although the leader accepts responsibility associated with his role...he seeks to minimize the influence of his hierarchical position. He is aware that trying to get results by pulling rank affects adversely the effectiveness of the group and his relationship with it."[12]

Examples of success using democratically oriented techniques are plentiful. By forming worker teams in the 1990s, the General Motors Pontiac Division increased productivity by 12 percent and achieved vast improvements in the spirit of cooperation between labor and management. Even more impressive results were obtained in the mid-1980s when the Ford Motor Co. broke the old mold of car development in giving birth to the Taurus model. Instead of having designers hand over their ideas to engineers, who then passed their conclusions on to manufacturing experts, who then built the kind of car the marketing people were told to sell, Ford started from scratch. Company executives gathered together some three hundred designers, engineers, manufacturing experts, and marketing staff and said, "Work together and give us a really great new automobile." This seemingly unwieldy body broke itself down into subgroups which met individually and together for many months. Top Ford people stayed out of the way, emerging only once in a while to inquire if everyone was getting support and the opportunity to give input. Their creation was the extraordinarily successful Taurus, which in 1992 finally overtook the Honda Accord as best-selling car in the United States. Until the design was retired in 2006, some seven million Tauruses were sold, along with several million of its lesser-known sister, the Mercury Sable.[13]

Linkert reports on a study in which five hundred clerical workers in a major company were divided into four subgroups, two of which operated under a highly participatory style of management, with teams making their own decisions, often by consensus, while the other two groups followed a strict, hierarchical, authoritarian style of management. After one year the hierarchically managed groups showed a 25 percent increase in productivity, and the participatory groups increased productivity by a slightly less 20 percent. Of more interest to the researchers were the sharp divergences in side effects: among the hierarchically managed groups, a measurable decrease in company loyalty, attitude, job interest, and work involvement was noted; among those that had the participatory experience, the outcome was exactly the opposite.

A Huge Step Forward

It is true the church does not manufacture automobiles or oversee large numbers of clerical workers. But it most certainly is in the business of facilitating healthy human relationships, assisting people to think clearly, and forming communities that can effect change in the larger world. The insights of modern management studies are surely adaptable to an institution with such objectives. In fact, popes have been talking about participation as essential in social and work groups throughout the twentieth century. Thus Pius XI in the 1920s: "We consider it more advisable... in the present condition of human society that... the work-contract be somewhat modified by a partnership contract... so that workers and employees become sharers in ownership or management." And thus John XXIII in the 1950s: "Workers should have an active role in the operation of the organization in which they are involved."[14]

This concern for broad participation is expressed especially in the papal emphasis on subsidiarity. The basic concept is that in any social system, decisions should be made at the lowest possible, appropriate level. This is how Pope John XXIII put it in the 1950s: "It is a fundamental principle of social philosophy... that one should not withdraw from individuals and commit to the community what they can accomplish by their own enterprise and industry. So too it is an injustice and... a grave evil... to transfer to the larger and higher collectivity functions which can be provided for by lesser and subordinate bodies." And it was a major theme with John Paul II in the 1990s: "Smaller social units, whether nations, communities, ethnic or racial groups, families or individuals, must not be namelessly absorbed into a greater conglomeration, thus having their prerogatives usurped."[15]

In political terms, says Nichols, subsidiarity means that "the federal government should not do what the state can do; the county should not take over the work of the city or village, nor the village of the neighborhood, nor the neighborhood of the family. The purpose of the larger social units is to aid and empower the lower, not to do their work for them, except in those rare cases where the lower, subsidiary social unit is dysfunctional." Adds Nichols, "It is characteristic of totalitarianism that a centralized power structure attempts to eliminate all subsidiary social groups that might provide opposition and to control individuals directly."[16]

Among ten principles approved by the synod of bishops in 1971 was a call for the church to put into practice the principle of subsidiarity in its own internal operation. But the 1983 Code of Canon Law failed to include any practical follow-ups on this. The application of subsidiarity to church governance would require radical change in policies from top to bottom. Yet the insistent call for decentralization of church decision making puts pressure on hierarchical leaders to practice what they preach. A call for decentralization is precisely a call for subsidiarity. Furthermore, Vatican II took a huge step toward broader participation within the church by its promotion of collegiality among the bishops, its insistence that the pope is a member of the same college with the other bishops, and its encouragement of participatory synods and councils at every level of the church community. The council also called for full participation of the faithful in parish and diocesan activities, including liturgical, financial, social, educational, and planning councils, committees, and other groups. These are bodies that can and do operate in a democratic way — up to a point.

The church's chronic problem with democracy is due in part to the right of dissent as a necessary ingredient in any democratic system. Before he became pope, Karol Wojtyla shared his favorable views on dissent:

> The structure . . . of a given society must be such as to allow the opposition that emerges from the soil of solidarity not only to express itself within the framework of the given community, but also to provide for its benefit.[17]

Yet after becoming the supreme pontiff, John Paul was outspoken in condemning dissent of any kind within the church and took punitive measures against theologians like Hans Küng and Charles Curran who dissented on matters of doctrine. Dissent on doctrine will be considered in detail in the next chapter. It should be noted in passing, however, that dissent on church teaching has a long and often honorable history of leading to the modification or complete withdrawal of certain doctrines. But there is no apparent reason why respectful dissent on matters of church governance (for example, the ordination of married men) could or should not be allowed, as John Paul said, so as "to express itself within the framework of the given community." There is nothing infallible about canon law. It has changed radically over the centuries and it will change again. Viewing the church over a period of centuries, I see then a battery of significant factors that point toward a democratic Catholic Church in the future:

- The church's historic aptitude for adapting to its own purposes various secular models of government.

- The church's retreat from a world-denying opposition toward every expression of the Enlightenment.

- The recognition of the secular world as God's creation and worthy of the believer's involvement in its development.

- The gradual endorsement of democratically organized labor unions, political parties, and constitutional governments, free elections, separation of church and state, and freedom of conscience.

* The promotion at the highest church levels of democratically related techniques such as subsidiarity and the encouragement of stronger participation of the laity in church affairs.

* The practical realization by church leaders that good people will not give their time and talent to organizations, even divinely instituted ones, that deny them a real voice in decision making.

Chapter Nine

The Church as a Democracy

✝

I am accustomed to lay great stress on the consensus fidelium [consensus of the faithful]. — JOHN HENRY NEWMAN

PERHAPS THE MOST IMPORTANT REASON for discussing the democratization of the Catholic Church is that the church is already democratic. In its essence, in its roots and foundation, in its very reason for existence, it is of the people, by the people, and for the people. That may come as a shock to those who prefer a lofty, esoteric religion mediated from high above, one that makes God unapproachably transcendent, God's representatives especially exalted, and God's creatures very small and childlike. But that is not what Catholicism was ever meant to be. The Second Vatican Council identified the whole church without distinction as "the People of God." Of course, this doesn't mean the church has always been true to its essence. The accounts narrated in earlier chapters reveal how the voice from below tends to get muffled from above.

In this I don't intend to present some novel theory at odds with established Catholic thought. I believe the notion of democracy has been implicit in the church's self-understanding all along and is only gradually being teased out of its history and theology and brought into the light. Theologians as different in time and style as John Henry Newman and Francis A. Sullivan, S.J., are among those who provide the basics of the concept.

I came upon both when studying the history of infallibility, a subject that had always puzzled and distressed me. Newman

I first encountered on a library shelf while looking for another author. Sullivan was suggested to me by a friend as the supreme authority on the nature of the church. From 1956 until 1992 he was professor of Catholic Ecclesiology at the Gregorian University in Rome. Many of his students there went on to become bishops in the U.S. church, among them Archbishop William Levada, who was named prefect of the Congregation for the Doctrine of the Faith, after the former prefect, Joseph Ratzinger, was elected pope in 2005.

Sullivan's flagship book is titled *Magisterium: Teaching Authority in the Catholic Church*. I delayed getting a copy for some time because the word "magisterium" reminded me of other overbearing words one runs into in church history, like "sovereignty" and "prepotency." When I read the book, I found it anything but offputting. His writing is dense but logical and persuasive. His understanding of authority is so balanced and sensible that I wanted to send copies of the book to some of the bishops (his former students) who, I'm convinced, missed his major insights. Before going more deeply into this, consider a few fundamentals that I think most Catholics can agree on:

First, the Incarnation means that God became human. He dwelt among us — ate, drank, worked, loved, died, and rose — in the human realm, and thereafter his followers would seek him principally in that realm. It was an angel who told his followers after the Ascension to stop gawking up into the sky: that is not where you will find him.

Second, Jesus sent the Holy Spirit to be with his people to the end of the ages. They were so filled with this presence that they acted with a confidence that was in no way justified by their worldly credentials — whether education, profession, or proven strength of character. This Spirit was not a gift exclusively for the apostles, disciples, and others gathered in the upper room. The Spirit was for the church, the whole church, the ongoing Body of Christ (and present too in the world even beyond the church). This was an emboldening Spirit that made it seem that carrying the good news to the ends of the world would be well worth the price.

Third, the People of God, in whom the Spirit dwells, have visible leaders, as they have had from the first days. These leaders, however chosen or designated over the centuries, have the responsibility to teach authoritatively what the church received from Jesus and what the church believes about God, Christ, and itself; they also must attempt to maintain this body in a kind of unity within the faith and with one another.

History shows this leadership, the hierarchy, to be susceptible to two major errors: first, to presume that this presence of the Holy Spirit justifies its authentic or definitive judgments without qualification, and second, to forget that the Spirit inheres in the whole Body, not just in those with leadership credentials. The solution to this chronic, twofold misunderstanding may well occur when the hierarchy confesses the sin of presumption and, for its penance, opens wide the windows of participation to the great mass of Christians, in whom the Spirit is also active. Or it may occur in another, maybe more dramatic way about which we can speculate later.

A "Listening" Magisterium

The Second Vatican Council went a long way toward opening the Catholic mind on these matters in the Dogmatic Constitution on Divine Revelation (*Dei Verbum*), no. 8:

> This tradition which comes to us from the apostles develops in the Church with the help of the Holy Spirit. For there is a growth in the understanding of the realities and the words which have been handed down. This happens through the contemplation and study made by believers, who treasure these things in their hearts, through the intimate understanding of spiritual things they experience, and through the preaching of those who have received through

episcopal succession the sure gift of truth. For as the centuries succeed one another, the Church constantly moves forward toward the fullness of divine truth until the words of God reach their complete fulfillment in her.

Notice the phrase, "there is a growth in the understanding." Everything has not been set out in a changeless order. There is "growth," the church "moves forward," and the movement is facilitated by — yes, the bishops — but first by "the contemplation and study of believers — that is, by the full church — and by their "understanding" and "experience." Notice too the movement is toward the "fullness" of truth. We haven't got it yet, because we can speak of God and the other realities of faith only by analogy — in words that reflect the limitations of our minds and the limitations of our time, culture, and conditioning. "Human propositions, particularly those which attempt to grasp and express divine reality," observes Sullivan, "can never do more than pick out some particular facet of the mystery, and say something, however imperfectly, about the particular aspect of the whole mystery." Nevertheless, he argues, "there is no reason to deny the very possibility that the Church could express its normative faith in propositions that are really true."[1]

Confidence about the truth of faith statements comes from a key passage in the Dogmatic Constitution on the Church (*Lumen Gentium*), no. 12:

> The body of the faithful as a whole, anointed as they are by the Holy Spirit, cannot err in matters of belief. Thanks to a supernatural sense of the faith which characterizes the People as a whole, it manifests this unerring quality when, from the bishops down to the last member of the laity, it shows universal agreement in matters of faith and morals. For, by this sense of faith which is aroused and sustained by the Spirit of truth, God's People accepts not the word of men but the very Word of God. It clings without fail to the faith once delivered to the saints, penetrates it more deeply by accurate insights, and applies it more thoroughly to life.

This is an astounding passage. It places the source of Catholic conviction about the truths of the faith first and foremost in "the People as a whole." That is where the Holy Spirit principally dwells, and that is where one must go initially to discern what is to be believed and what isn't. Vatican II speaks in detail about the ability of the bishops to speak infallibly in certain situations and the unique ability of the pope to do so. But the ground of their gifts is in the Body from the top "to the last member of the laity." This would seem to put a huge obligation on the part of the teachers, the magisterium, to be attentive to what the Body of the church thinks and believes. That is the home of the faith. Vatican II puts it this way in *Dei Verbum* (no. 10)

> Now the Magisterium is not above the Word of God, but serves it, teaching only what has been handed on, listening to it devoutly, guarding it conscientiously, and explaining it faithfully, by divine commission and with the help of the Holy Spirit.

The magisterium is not free to teach whatever it agrees on among its members; it must present only what has been "handed down" to the church in its teaching, life, and worship. The emphasis of the church as bearer of the Word, says Sullivan, "is a salutary corrective to the notion found in earlier treatises on the subject, according to which the deposit of faith was entrusted uniquely to the successors of the apostles and is handed on primarily, if not exclusively, in the official teaching of the magisterium."[2]

Listening to the Word, Sullivan explains, means bishops "must first be hearers of the Word; before they can belong to the 'teaching church' . . . they have to belong to the 'learning church.' And since the 'sacred deposit of the Word of God' has been entrusted to the Church, it follows that the bishops have to listen devoutly to this Word as it is handed on from generation to generation."[3] What they are required to listen to is the tradition of the church. In a crucial passage in his book on consulting the faithful, Newman presents his perspective:

I think I am right in saying that the tradition of the Apostles, committed to the whole Church in its various constituents and functions, manifests itself variously at various times: sometimes by the mouth of the episcopacy, sometimes by the doctors, sometimes by the people, sometimes by liturgies, rites, ceremonies, and customs, by events, disputes, movements, and all those other phenomena which are comprised under the name of history. It follows that none of these channels of tradition may be treated with disrespect; granting at the same time fully, that the gift of discerning, discriminating, defining, promulgating, and enforcing any portion of that tradition resides solely in the *Ecclesia docens* [the teaching church]. One man will lay more stress on one aspect of doctrine, another on another; for myself, I am accustomed to lay great stress on the *consensus fidelium* [consensus of the faithful].[4]

G. K. Chesterton is often cited for his pithy saying that "tradition is the democracy of the dead." That is, it is found in those believers over the centuries who contributed to the various manifestations Newman speaks of; they placed their votes, so to speak, in the times in which they lived, and their accepted contributions have become our tradition. But Chesterton was not correct, insofar as he was talking about the church. Tradition does not stop at some point in the past. It continues in the living Body of Christ today and will do so into the future. This ongoing aspect of tradition has too often been overlooked by the magisterium, even treated with disrespect.

Newman's tendency to lay "great stress on the consensus of the faithful" came from his study of the Arian heresy of the fourth century, discussed in chapter 3. At that time the consensus operated in open contradiction to the great majority of the bishops, the church's official teachers. In the end it prevented the Arian interpretation of Jesus' nature from being accepted and passed into church tradition. The faithful at that time, it might be said, exercised their franchise (with the help of the Holy Spirit) and thus changed history.

There is then a democratic dynamic in the church's self-awareness. The obvious question today is whether the magisterium is aware of this dynamic. It appears that on many issues, for example, the prohibition of contraception, the teaching authority prefers Chesterton's definition and does not want to hear or discuss what the sense or consensus of the living and breathing faithful today might be on the subject.

A "Listening" Papacy

This requirement of hearing and learning is not limited to bishops, in Sullivan's analysis. It applies to the deliberations of general councils and especially to the pope when he is preparing to propose a dogma. Since the deposit of the faith has been given to the whole church, says Sullivan,

> it follows that before the pope can define a dogma he must listen to the Church, and he can define as dogma only what he finds in the faith of the Church. The pope has no source of revelation that is independent of the faith-life of the Church. It follows that the pope simply cannot define a dogma without having in some real way consulted the faith of the Church, for he can define as dogma only something that has been and is being handed on in the teaching, life and worship of the Church.[5]

Sullivan rarely gets as explicit about this interactive view of doctrine as he does in the above passage. He wants the message to be very clear. "The role of the faithful is seen to be not merely passive obedience to formal authority," he explains, "but an active sharing in the process by which the whole People of God clings without fail to the faith once delivered to the saints."[6]

As one who studied ecclesiology in the middle of the last century, I never heard one word about any of this. The role of the faithful, we were told, is exclusively a passive one; it never occurred to us in the seminary that teaching came in any other way than vertically — from God, to the pope, to the bishops, to the priests, and finally to the humble laity. Even today, one rarely hears even a hint from bishops or priests about such a different theological emphasis. I wonder how many Catholics are aware of it and its implications.

A big consideration is how this absolutely necessary consultation can and should take place. In the only two cases when popes specifically invoked their infallibility in proclaiming dogmas (the doctrines of the Immaculate Conception and Mary's Assumption into heaven), they did perform prior consultations of the world's bishops, who presumably were in touch with the beliefs of their people on these matters. In this admittedly remote way the priests and laity may be said to have voted their approval. The requirement does not mean, notes Sullivan, that the decision on a dogma or any other church teaching should be determined only by a worldwide opinion poll. The democracy of the dead, that is, the two-thousand-year legacy of tradition on the subject, must also be taken into account, along with what Scripture has to say about the proposed teaching. Sullivan believes there is a variety of ways a pope can consult, but "given the ease of world-wide consultation provided by modern means of communication, a pope could hardly be said in the future to have fulfilled his grave obligation...if he neglected to consult the episcopal college about the doctrine he contemplated defining."[7]

Given the educational level of Catholics in this century, he would also fail in his obligation if there was not a substantial consultation of the laity. And in view of the achievements of the ecumenical movement, it seems to me, there would have to be in addition some consultation with the Orthodox Catholic churches and with the Protestant churches, which Vatican II recognizes as preserving elements which can "provide access to the community of salvation."[8]

The expected response to defined doctrine, whether from a pope or a general council, is "reception" by the faithful through a sincere act of faith. Yet so serious are the requirements of consultation that Sullivan concurs with theologian B. C. Butler in saying, "If a definition failed in the end to enjoy such a reception on the part of the Church, this would prove that the definition had not in fact met the stringent requirements for an [infallible] pronouncement."[9] A similar view was expressed by Joseph Ratzinger in 1969, some years before he became pope: "Where there is neither consensus on the part of the universal Church nor clear testimony in the sources," he said, "no binding decision is possible. If such a decision were formally made, it would lack the necessary conditions and the question of the decision's legitimacy would have to be examined."[10]

To prevent conscientious Catholics from getting entangled in too many theological technicalities, Sullivan points out that they may always avail themselves of Canon 749.3 of the 1983 code, which says, "No doctrine is understood to have been dogmatically defined unless this is manifestly the case."[11]

He also calls attention to the idea, presented in Vatican II's Decree on Ecumenism (no. 11) that there exists a "hierarchy of truths" in Catholic teaching, since "they vary in their relationship to the foundation of the Christian faith." Many Catholics, he notes, tend to place papal infallibility near the top of their belief system since it has gotten so much attention since its exaltation at the First Vatican Council. "But the sober fact is that it is far from being among the truths at the very foundation of our faith," declares Sullivan.

> It would be a gross misunderstanding to think that the certitude of our Catholic faith somehow depends on the infallibility of the pope.... Actually, our belief in the infallibility of the pope is a fairly remote consequence of our foundational belief that Jesus is the Lord, and that he loved the Church and gave himself up for her.[12]

Developing an Informed Conscience

The democratic aspect of the church has relevance also regarding the reception or non-reception of authoritative but not infallibly proposed teaching. Non-reception has become something of an epidemic since Pope Paul VI's 1968 encyclical *Humanae Vitae,* and it has spread to other clearly enunciated church teachings on homosexuality, remarriage after divorce, in vitro fertilization, and stem-cell research, to cite some of the better-known battlegrounds.

Virtually everyone today is aware that some official doctrines have at times been found to be erroneous and were then substantially altered or discarded. Examples include the church's long toleration of slavery; its decidedly condemnatory attitude toward non-believers, especially Jews; the ban on taking any interest on a loan; the absolute prohibition against divorce; the teaching that the earth is the center of the universe; and the condemnation of freedom of religion. Most of these teachings had been in place for centuries; some were regarded as unchangeable, even infallible, dogmas, because of their long, unbroken history in Catholic tradition. They all, however, gave way in time to newer thinking or new discoveries. People know this and they also know what follows: If the Catholic Church has erred in the past, it can err in the future — or more to the point — it can err in the present. One of the best known of these reversals was Vatican II's declaration in 1966 that everyone has a right to freedom of religion, a position considered unthinkable well into the twentieth century.

The position that all forms of artificial contraception are intrinsically evil and may never be allowed regardless of circumstance is another case in point. Only in the 1950s did contrary opinions to that position first appear. Then with the development of the birth control pill, theologians, medical specialists, and a great throng of laity began to press hard for a revocation of the doctrine. In the 1960s a special commission formed by Pope John XXIII to advise him on the issue met, studied, debated, conducted their own survey of married Catholic couples, and reached by vote a nearly unanimous conclusion: the absolute prohibition of contraception should be rescinded. This birth control commission was, incidentally, an interesting, though very limited, model of papal consultation in action. Before it finished its work, the membership included bishops, priests, theologians, doctors, psychiatrists, psychologists, population experts, and even three married couples. But in 1968 Pope Paul VI, who had succeeded Pope John, rejected the commission findings, fearing any change on the teaching would lead down the slippery slope toward moral relativity.

It would be a grave understatement to say the encyclical was not well received. After its release, there were protests all over the world by leading moral theologians, priests, bishops, and even some national bishop conferences (not in the United States). A large number of Catholics have left the church because of the decision. And polls consistently show upward of 80 percent of those who identify themselves as Catholics to be in opposition to the official norm on contraception — for almost forty years. Clearly, an overwhelming proportion of the Catholic population has not "received" the teaching. They have been voting no and continue to do so. John Henry Newman's own analysis of the Arian controversy in the fourth century convinced him that any doctrine, even one supported by the great mass of the church's bishops, the official teachers, becomes irrelevant and meaningless if it does not meet with "reception" from the body of the church. Without reception, the doctrine would be like a tree falling in a forest with no one present. It would have no effect. It was this realization that led Newman to put "great stress" on the consensus of the faithful as perhaps the most reliable indicator of what is and what is not reliable teaching. Though he did not use the word "democratic," he was, in effect, placing a heavy, preferential, democratic confidence in the people's judgment enlightened by the Holy Spirit.

Today, theologians like Sullivan do not conclude, however, that disputed positions can be simply ignored by Catholics. Out of consideration for the church's teaching authority generally, they should attempt what the church calls a religious "submission [*obsequium* in the original Latin of canon law] of mind and will" to teachings — like the one on contraception, recognizing at the same time the possibility that this norm may be flawed. They should, in other words, remember that the Catholic Church over the centuries has passed on to the generations the fundamental truths one lives by if one is a Catholic,; and is therefore entitled to respect, even the benefit of the doubt. Other theologians would argue that "submission" is too strong a word and that *obsequium* might be more accurately rendered "due respect." In any event, Sullivan says:

> it would be inconsistent for the magisterium to propose a moral norm as a requirement of the natural law [as it does in the case of contraception] ...and not offer convincing reasons that would appeal to the intelligence of those to whom this teaching is directed. When the norm itself is said to be discoverable by human reasoning, it would be a mistake to rely too heavily on merely formal authority in proposing it for acceptance by thinking people. In such a case it would surely not be surprising if for many of the faithful the formal authority of the magisterium did not suffice to overcome the doubt that remained in their minds concerning the truth of the official teaching.[13]

On that basis, he concludes that "if in a particular instance, Catholics have offered their religious submission of mind and will to the authority of the magisterium by making an honest and sustained effort to achieve internal assent to its teaching, and still find that doubts about its truths remain so strong in their minds that they cannot actually give their sincere intellectual assent to it, I do not see how one could judge such non-assent, or internal dissent, to involve any lack of obedience to the magisterium. Having done all that they were capable of doing towards achieving assent, they actually fulfilled their obligation of obedience."[14] By sincerely and prayerfully developing an informed conscience on the subject, such persons can hardly then be accused of being "cafeteria Catholics."

Indeed, many Catholics have left the church over the contraception ruling, the ban against ordination of women, or the official stand on homosexuality, believing their non-assent excludes them from participation in the church and reception of the sacraments. They may not be aware of the range of theological opinion on these matters that exists in the church today. They probably have not heard from the pulpit on Sunday or read in their diocesan newspaper that they must, with guidance and prayer, form their own conscience and use their own judgment in deciding. On the contrary, they have heard from official sources over and over that dissent on any church doctrine is heresy or apostasy. I fear many see themselves as passive subjects of a dictatorial authority that may never be contradicted, whether at the Vatican, diocesan, or parish level.

Meanwhile — and here is the future — there is a growing majority: Catholics who dissent on certain official positions, yet attend Mass regularly, receive communion, participate actively in their parishes, and nevertheless sleep soundly at night. These Catholics have some awareness of the theological nuances, and they are certain they may act, must act, with an informed conscience. They may have thought, prayed, and worked this all out on their own. Or they may have talked to a priest in the parish or discussed it with lay friends, or they may have read articles and books on the subject. I think they understand the intrinsic democracy of the Catholic Church, that they are required to be what Vatican II called them to be, a fully adult church — "the People of God." Knowing that, they operate with the kind of freedom that is theirs as members of the church.

Chapter Ten

A Convergence of Crises

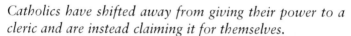

Catholics have shifted away from giving their power to a cleric and are instead claiming it for themselves.

— DAVID GIBSON

WHAT ACTION WOULD YOU TAKE if you were a major stockholder in a large company that had the following characteristics?

* Skilled managers are leaving the company in large numbers before reaching retirement age, and top leadership, despite great effort, is unable to interest enough young recruits even to enter the management training program.

* Customers are increasingly uninterested in the company product, some taking their business elsewhere, some declining to visit the company showrooms, some publicly expressing their anger and outrage at management.

* The company is currently paying out more than a billion dollars to settle lawsuits filed by customers whose children were sexually abused by company managers over the years.

* Several branches of the company have declared bankruptcy and others are expected to take similar steps in the next few years.

* Top executives admit the problems are serious but insist they are unable to move in new directions because established policy reserves all upper-level decisions exclusively to the company's president.

You would of course consider selling your stock before it's too late, recognizing that there is only one word for this bizarre confluence of negative indicators: crisis! The "company" is the U.S. Catholic Church (though the situation isn't all that different in Catholic churches elsewhere in the world). I believe the ongoing nature of this crisis is so severe and so debilitating that it will eventually compel major structural changes in the church's operational system. Whether the changes come from above or from below or from a combination of both remains to be seen. Thus far, hierarchical efforts have been largely to treat the symptoms, but inevitably the source must be confronted, just as cancer can never be cured by just addressing symptoms.

The Perfect Storm

It all happened so suddenly and without warning that no one was ready. In the mid-1950s Catholic seminaries were full of young men preparing for the priesthood. Large dioceses were churning out thirty-five or more fresh, young, anointed heads a year, and religious orders, male and female, were experiencing similar bonanzas. The church was in a building boom, erecting or enlarging seminaries, novitiates, motherhouses, and residential facilities for the tide of youth that just kept coming. Then suddenly in the 1960s the balloon burst — or better, it began leaking and the leak just goes on and on. Today the countryside is dotted with many of these structures, which have been transformed into lay retreat centers, residences for elderly nuns or priests, or administrative offices. Others have been sold to other Christian denominations, to other religious faiths, or to secular businesses, universities, and schools. The famed Culinary Institute of America in Hyde Park, New York, for example, is housed in a once flourishing former Jesuit novitiate. Still other structures stand empty, with long gaping halls, small bedrooms and dusty chapels awaiting the demolition ball.

At about the same time priests and sisters at work in parishes and schools all over the country began to resign or to seek dispensation from their vows in large numbers. Statistics on the mass exodus of priests are notoriously imprecise. This is due in part to the fact that dioceses tend to over-report their priests' population by listing as "on leave" some who have left ministry altogether or by mistakenly including as "active" priests who have retired or are dead. But whatever the source, statistics over the past forty years are consistent in that all point in a decidedly downward direction. Perhaps the most accurate information was uncovered by sociologist Richard Schoenherr, who made a career of double and triple checking the data, going diocese by diocese and priest by priest. In the 1993 book *Full Pews and Empty Altars,* Schoenherr and co-author Lawrence Young predicted a 40 percent decline in the number of active diocesan priests over the forty-year period from 1966 to 2005. The 1966 total of 35,000 diocesan priests, they predicted, would dwindle to 21,000 by 2005. As it turned out, they were a bit too optimistic, since the 21,000 figure was realized in 2003, two years ahead of schedule. The overall loss, said the authors, was due to a combination of events: the remarkable decrease in ordinations (a 50 percent decline over the span), an unprecedented increase in priest resignations, and the steady pace of priest retirements and deaths.[1]

During that same forty-year period the U.S. Catholic population was growing from 47 million to 67 million. The shrinking of the clergy meant an ever increasing gap in the ratio of priests to the Catholic population. It meant an increasingly older clergy population (in 1985 the average age of priests was forty-six, and in 2005 it was sixty). The trend has also resulted in the closing of many parishes, the merger of others, and the growing phenomenon of priestless parishes, with a layperson, often a religious sister, serving as administrator.

Meanwhile, the decrease in women religious was even more precipitous. In 1965 there were 181,000 religious sisters (active and retired), according to the most reliable data. Ten years later the figure was 130,000, a loss of 50,000 sisters in just one de-cade. In the mid-2000s religious sisters number about 75,000, representing a decrease of 58 percent over the forty-year period. The average age of the remaining sisters is seventy and rising. The implications have been stark for Catholic parochial schools once staffed almost exclusively by sisters. The change gravely affected other Catholic institutions, including high schools, hos-pitals, orphanages, and social service agencies. For those who remained in service, this historic departure "looms in the mem-ory of sisters and ex-sisters with the vividness of an earthquake," according to journalist Kenneth Briggs. He cited one Franciscan nun, a postulant in 1981, who said, "Everyone seemed to be go-ing out the door when I was coming in. It was traumatic." Adds Briggs, "What had been a bedrock of stable routine and a clus-ter of constant companions became, instead, a vista of shifting sands and vanishing soul mates."[2] For priests who stayed the trauma was similar, and it had a contagious effect. Many began to wonder why they were standing in place when it looked like almost everybody was on the way out.

To the larger Catholic population it seemed as if some noxious vapor had wafted into the environment, sapping the dedica-tion and vitality of those who had committed themselves to the church. What's this all about? they wondered. Why so many, why now? As one who resigned from the active priesthood in 1970, I have thought a lot about this, talked to others, and read what the experts have had to say. The exodus was caused by an array of factors intersecting all at once — a kind of "perfect storm" that can occur only when a collection of unlikely events just happen to converge. It was due to the emergence of the middle class. Once happily secluded in their safe religious and ethnic ghettos, Catholic families were breaking out and moving on up — out to the suburbs, on up to better-paying jobs and col-lege education for the children, coming into close contact with Protestants, Jews, even atheists. The world seemed so much big-ger. No longer did religious life appear, as it once did, as the one accessible road to a meaningful life and respectability in the community.

It was due to Vatican II. By breaking down the centuries-old distinction between the exalted vocation of the professional religious and the lowly stance of the worldly laity, the council created a kind of new, even playing field. Marriage was no longer seen as the catch-all for those lesser souls who had not received a higher calling. Holiness was equally available to all.

It was due to *Humanae Vitae,* the 1968 papal encyclical that ruled that all forms of artificial contraception are immoral and forbidden. For priests the encyclical was a disturbing development. Many, if not most, had come to believe the ban was about to be lifted. When it was instead reaffirmed, they found themselves in agreement with Charles Curran and other theologians who dissented. Yet these priests, as official representatives of the church, were expected to publicly uphold an official teaching that touched so intimately on the lives of married couples. Unwilling to do so, many resigned.

It was the obligation of lifelong celibacy. The church's traditional teachings on sexuality were under assault on several fronts from the 1960s on. The requirement of celibacy came to be seen as supportive of an anti-body, anti-world mentality. More importantly, it was attacked as the very foundation of clericalism and the exclusive concentration of power in the church to males. When rumors that the church would soon allow a married clergy were thwarted soon after Vatican II, priests (and sisters) began to seriously reevaluate their commitments.

It was the intransigence of church superiors. For religious sisters in particular, the years immediately following the council offered hitherto undreamt of possibilities: for upgrading their rules and regulations, for advanced education, for moving into new and varied ministries, for giving voice to the feminine character of the church. In all these areas there were and are many success stories. There are also limitless accounts of the heavy hand of authority (whether from the Vatican, the diocese, or the order itself) squelching such ambition. The assumption that most sisters left principally to get married is not supported by data. A 1966 study of women's orders indicated that only 20 percent of those in final vows who left did so in order to marry, while "unhappiness with community life" was listed as the major reason. Says journalist Briggs, "A broad consensus shows that what affected sisters much more than the appeals of marriage, family and sex was the perception that Church authority was too heavy-handed, oppressive and inhibiting."[3]

Together, all these factors weave in and out of each other, but it's not difficult to perceive a common thread: frustration with an authority that failed to implement the progressive initiatives it had committed itself to at Vatican II.

More conservative voices dismiss the great exodus as past history and point to the new religious orders of women, which have returned to the full religious habit and a submissive lifestyle consistent with that of religious orders in past centuries. They appear to be the only orders attracting new members. They also point to the handful of dioceses (Lincoln, Nebraska; Arlington, Virginia; and Denver, Colorado, for example) that have large numbers of seminarians. This is the real wave of the future, declare their supporters. Those flourishing orders and dioceses get a lot of media attention precisely because they are so unusual. But they are so few in number and so contrarian in approach, they do not represent more than a splash. Catholicism is big enough to embrace many expressions of spirituality and theology. And nostalgia for the past always accompanies new developments as a kind of brake, but I do not believe it is the direction of the future.

Rethinking the Faith

When you enter a Catholic church on Sunday morning, the situation does not look especially alarming. There's a priest at the altar (usually) and a dutiful, respectful congregation in the pews, making some effort to participate. Theologian Richard McBrien says it is more than likely that these parishioners are liberal in their religious views because these constitute the great majority of today's active Catholics:

> Many were formed by Vatican II and others have grown up in a Church shaped by it. Like the council itself, they hold that the Church is the People of God and that they — women and men alike — have an integral role to play in its mission and ministries. They are generally happy with the liturgy as renewed and reformed by the council, except perhaps for some of the homilies and music. But they would not want to return to the Latin Mass or to a style of worship focused on the priest rather than the whole congregation.[4]

While this may be generally true, there is nevertheless a steady hemorrhaging occurring in this broad cross-section, and there is likewise a changing perception among those who remain of what it means to be Catholic. For church leaders there is more than enough cause for alarm here. A 2006 poll by the American Religious Identification Survey revealed that 43 percent of those claiming no religious affiliation are former Catholics and that Catholics are departing the church at a rate higher than that in any other denomination or religion. Earlier polls have been reporting notable dropout increases for years.

An immediate rejoinder to these negative indicators is the simple fact that the U.S. Catholic population is showing real growth, by several million people, on an annual basis. However, the growth statistics are misleading. First, unlike other Christian denominations, the Catholic Church tends to consider every baptized Catholic as a member even if that person has had no contact with the church for many years — "once a Catholic, always a Catholic." As a result, many ex-Catholics may be listed on parish roles forever unless they specifically notify the church of their new affiliation or non-affiliation. Second, the reported growth is overwhelmingly due to Hispanic immigration to this country and the high Latino-American birth rate over the past forty years. But recent studies show that Latinos are now leaving Catholicism to join Pentecostal and evangelical churches at astounding rates, as many as half a million a year. Studies also show that many other Latinos drop out, especially in the second and third generation, and join no other faith community.

The worrisome dropout phenomenon is accompanied by a substantial shift in what the great mass of Catholics still believe about their religion. Sociologist Dean Hoge, who has conducted numerous surveys of Catholics over several decades, finds that the boundaries of belief "are now fairly vague and porous, and they are slowly becoming more so over time." In his 2005 Center of Catholic Identity Study, he found that between 65 and 75 percent of Catholics believe you "can be a good Catholic" without obeying the church's teaching about divorce and remarriage, without obeying church teaching on birth control, and without going to church on Sunday. Some 58 percent said you can also be a good Catholic without obeying church teaching on abortion (the figure was 89 percent among those under thirty-five). On the other hand, only a minority said you can be a good Catholic without believing Jesus physically rose from the dead or without believing that the bread and wine actually become the body and blood of Jesus in the Mass.[5]

Hoge also listed twelve elements of Catholicism and asked the respondents which they considered most important, somewhat important, and not very important. Between 76 and 84 percent listed helping the poor, belief in Jesus' resurrection, and the sacraments as very important, while less than 42 percent considered church teaching against the death penalty, the teaching authority of the Vatican, and a celibate male clergy as very important. Among young Catholics only 11 percent considered these last three items very important.

It appears, says Hoge, that Catholics remain committed (more or less) to the basic doctrines of the creed but increasingly uncommitted regarding moral issues and even the right of the church to rule authoritatively on such issues. Other studies have shown that Catholic attendance at Sunday Mass, which stood at about 75 percent thirty years ago, has dropped to about 32 percent in the new century. "Across the board, on issues ranging from homosexuality to sex outside of marriage to remarrying without an annulment," says journalist David Gibson, "Catholics have shifted away from giving their power to a cleric and are instead claiming it for themselves."[6]

I do not think it's a stretch to say that underneath the numbers, a great many Catholics deeply resent their lack of a voice in the church. In response, they refuse to conform to dictates that come down unilaterally from above; they want to participate, especially in decisions that relate directly to their lives and experience, yet few have hope this can ever happen.

This is more and more true among young Catholics. During my years as a journalism professor at Northwestern University, I have discussed religious affiliation with many students, most often those in programs I've overseen on religion and media issues. Rare indeed is the Catholic student who acknowledges without qualification a Catholic identity. Some will say, "I was, uh, raised as a Catholic," or "I used to be a Catholic" or even "I'm a recovering Catholic." When I inquire what this means, they can be forthright in explaining their position. "The church isn't interested in me or what I think" is a common response, or "I guess I've just lost interest," or "I've outgrown the Catholic Church," or "I can't accept a church that still sees women as second-class citizens." And of course there is the popular "I'm-spiritual-but-not-religious-now" response.

To be sure, there are also students who are quite open about their disagreements with the church, yet are struggling to be faithful and seeking wisdom and support from friends in the campus Catholic community. I have encountered too some who identify themselves as "John Paul II Catholics," who are happily conservative in their beliefs, extremely obedient to church authority, and pious in ways that might even embarrass their devout Catholic grandparents. It is largely from these that the new religious communities and a handful of dioceses are finding recruits. They are atypical of most young Catholics who are tentative in their allegiance to the church and ambiguous at best about their relationship with it.

Theologian Tom Beaudoin, who has written widely on young Catholics, says they often find the post–Vatican II church

> a place of self-deception, abusive silence, and double-talk, especially about sexuality and about power.... How many of us know young adults who are waiting for a credible, believable church, a church that addresses real life issues, a church that treats us like adults, that takes our cultures seriously, a church that feeds us spiritually, that asks our gifts?[7]

Women on the Verge

If there is any group church leadership cannot afford to alienate, it is Catholic women. For centuries they have been the can-do enablers, the backbone of church life. At the center of the family, the domestic church, they remain the principal passers-on of the faith to their children and grandchildren. They do the critical work in parishes as schoolteachers and organizers of virtually all the social, educational, and recreational activity. They constitute the vast majority of today's lay ministers and lay volunteers, assuming services once relegated solely to the clergy. Polls show that women are far more apt than men to say that religion is important to them, more faithful in attendance at Mass, more likely to have close friends among parish members. It is no exaggeration to say that without women, the church would collapse overnight as a stable social entity.

Yet Catholic women today are deeply troubled, alienated, frustrated, resentful, and in some cases hostile toward the church as an institution. Some have left, some have taken a stand in the forefront of church reform, others continue their generous service as before, hiding their bitterness behind a polite smile. Burnout is not an uncommon experience.

"I would never encourage anyone to leave the Roman Catholic Church," says Deborah Halter, an author, journalist, and activist for change, "but I simply cannot keep seeing less and less of Jesus in the upper echelons of church hierarchy and re-main a healthy Christian. . . . I have carried with me the faith but not the institution of my heritage. I mourn the stillborn hopes of Vatican II but do not feel compelled to spend another 25 years struggling for their revivification."[8]

"I believe I am in the church too," says Genevieve O'Hara, a former sister who traces her disillusionment to the time she stood in St. Peter's Square at the Vatican watching a phalanx of priests distributing communion — not a single woman allowed to help. "But I take no part in a lot of the nonsense — the hierarchical structure, the concentration of power. I think that's really, really wrong. So I am outside of it."[9]

For many the sense of second-class citizenship came in midlife after decades of accepting the rules and doctrines of the church as non-negotiable givens. In Paige Byrne Shortal's case, something happened one day at Mass as she recited the creed. . . . For us men and for our salvation he came down. . . . "For us men," she says. "I couldn't get past it." She began a list of the obvious things she had just overlooked: "The church was all about men. The scriptures were written by men, interpreted by men and about men. The popes were men, as were the bishops, priests and the spiritual directors I knew. The laws were written by men, interpreted by men, enforced by men. The prayers were prayed by men. And of course God was a 'he' and 'he' sent 'his' son. At that time the Spirit to me was an 'it.' Two men and a bird."[10]

What was it that triggered this awakening? I think it can be traced in large part to the same "perfect storm" of events that led to the departures and alienations discussed earlier in this chapter. The biggest of these factors was surely Vatican II. It created such hopes that many entered a state of euphoria, while also opening eyes to the serious humbug aspects of the church. Jeannette Batz, a *National Catholic Reporter* journalist, wrote in 2001,

> After Vatican II many Catholic women were convinced that change would soon be blowing through that open window, the aggiornamento promised by Pope John XXIII. They'd

be ordained alongside their brethren, and the hierarchy would fade into an egalitarian, communitarian church of the people. Over three decades that hope turned to anger. And now even the anger has burned away. Nobody expects change anytime soon. If and when it does come, activists worry that it won't be a change born of repentance, but rather expediency wrung from the shortage of celibate male priests.[11]

Unquestionably, the denial of priestly ordination to women was the largest source of female disillusionment. It became the major target for activists after the council. But it was not the only target, and for many women it's not even the main one.

The council took place when the feminist movement was making deep inroads in American society. The era of patriarchy, male domination, was technically over, and the call everywhere was for women's equality: in business, commerce, politics, education, the media — and religion. This was more than an it's-our-turn-now call. It was the dawning recognition that inequality hadn't just cheated women out of what was rightfully theirs; it had cheated everyone of the unique gifts women have as women. Women's potential contribution in the area of pastoring in the Catholic Church appeared enormous. Their skills in developing interpersonal relationships, in fostering inclusion in social situations rather than exclusion, in valuing the importance of human experience in making important discussions — all this is so compatible with what pastoring is all about that it's almost a job description. According to Margaret Murphy, author of *How Catholic Women Have Changed,* "Women's charisms, women's energies seem uniquely to fit them for ministry of this kind, which is responsive to the anxieties, losses and burdens that people bear in life."[12]

If in the years after Vatican II, the hierarchy had given women a pledge that these pastoral charisms would be put to wider use and that "full participation" in ministry would at least be considered at some future date, the frustration and alienation might have been assuaged. Instead, the Vatican responded by issuing a salvo of documents explaining why women as priests is out of the question: because only men were present at the Last Supper (probably not true), because women were never ordained in the church (much disputed on the basis of historical evidence), and because women do not "resemble Jesus" in his maleness (a source of very bad jokes). Pope John Paul declared the matter closed in the 1990s and forbade any further conversation about the subject.

For those on the verge of departure, all this accelerated their decision. Others found relief in the development of women's liturgies employing prayers, symbols and signs, music, and the breaking of bread in a spirit nurturing their own sense of the sacred. In this they were aided by Catholic feminist scholars like Rosemary Ruether, who wrote in the mid-1980s:

> Women in contemporary churches are suffering from linguistic and eucharistic famine. They can no longer nurture their souls in alienating words that ignore or systematically deny their existence. They are starved for the words of life, for symbolic forms that fully and wholeheartedly affirm their personhood.... They desperately need primary communities that journey into wholeness, rather than constantly negating and thwarting it.[13]

Such communities with no organizational relation to the institutional church have spread quietly and widely in homes, convents, and hospitable Protestant churches.

The U.S. Catholic Bishops Conference in the early 1980s began planning to offer an olive branch in the form of a pastoral letter on women. For almost ten years they consulted with some seventy-five thousand women across the country and finally produced a draft that was affirming of women's equality and condemnatory toward sexism. However, when the document went to Rome (for the necessary approval), the Vatican found it unacceptable and required a revision that would shift the focus to the evils of contraception and the ban on women's ordination. In 1992, after a hot debate, the dispirited bishops' conference voted to scrap the pastoral letter on women and ceased attempting to publish strong directives on any subject for the next ten years — until the abuse crisis hit.

The Collapse of a Feudal System

Even if the chronic problems discussed here were the only ones afflicting the church, one would have to conclude that a major overhaul is in order. When you add to the list that more recent catastrophe — the priest abuse scandal — it's obvious (at least to the outside world) that an overhaul is mandatory. It is hard to imagine anything more disillusioning or outrageous than this betrayal of trust by priests and bishops. Although it involved directly only a relatively small minority of priests (and a few religious sisters), with the incidents spread over four decades, the revelations, beginning in 2002 and going on and on and on, aroused the anger of the entire nation. This was a story ready-made for the media — a combination of religion, sex, violence, secrecy, hush money, and crass hypocrisy by the presumed paragons of moral rectitude.

At first public indignation was directed at the priests responsible. Then, as more information came to the surface, the public realized the involvement of bishops in hiding allegations, moving guilty priests from parish to parish without informing pastors or parishioners, and persuading victims and their families not to file criminal or civil charges. There seemed to be no limit to what some bishops would do in order not to cause "scandal." Ironically, all of this was setting the scene for the worst scandal in U.S. Catholic Church history. It has undermined the most valuable possession bishops have: their claim on legitimate authority. According to theologian Gerard Mannion:

> We are faced with a crisis of confidence in the church, which by and large stems from a crisis of confidence in the ecclesial authorities, in terms of their style, organization, actual

leadership, and personnel. It is a crisis whereby the authority of many church leaders is now perceived to have been abused, lost, abdicated, or simply removed.... Church leaders are increasingly perceived as no longer having any claim to legitimate authority and leadership, and yet many church policies are shaped by the mistaken assumption that blind obedience and automatic deference continue to exist.[14]

Yet the abuse scandal provides a supremely important benefit. It dramatically lifts a veil to reveal the big problem behind the other problems. It is a kind of epiphany, a shocking manifestation of what is really wrong. It's a falling of the scales from the eyes of the blind. It's a prism through which anyone can focus on the message that history and current events are trying to convey: without wide participation, without voice and democratization, the church is unable to be its true self — a credible sign of the Kingdom of God. For many this was the first time they got the message.

Reflecting on the intensity of public reaction to the abuse phenomenon, journalist Peter Steinfels asks a probing question and gives an incisive answer:

> Why did Catholics show so little patience for distinctions between the policies of different bishops of dioceses; between different time periods and the changing social and therapeutic views that prevailed in each of them; between degrees of offenses; between blunt efforts to block prosecution, settlements, or publicity and much more complicated and arguably legitimate actions to avoid prolonged litigation, respect reputations, and protect confidentiality? The truth is the scandal ignited the accumulated frustration of millions of ordinary Catholics, liberal and conservative, who had become increasingly convinced that their concerns and experience were not being taken into account.[15]

"Not being taken into account..." because that's not the way feudal systems operate. To grasp the situation today it is useful, I think, to view the church as the last deeply rooted feudal system of the Western world.

This form of government, which dominated civil life in Europe for almost seven hundred years, was based on a strict, hierarchical pyramid, with a king at the top. Below him was a layer of lords and beneath the lords a core of vassals. On the bottom were the serfs, who toiled in the fields. The serfs did not question the vassals nor the vassals the lords, nor the lords the king. Command and control were exercised from the top down. Loyalty and obedience were expected from the bottom up. It was a patriarchal, male-dominated, military model. There was little accountability from those on the upper levels toward those on the lower ones; there were no checks or balances. Apology to those below was never in order, and the concept of transparency in dealings had not yet evolved.

When complaints occurred or problems developed, the first question was not "who has been offended and why?" but "what must we do to keep the system intact and stable?" A revolt at any level could bring down this whole house of cards.

Jesus was operating in a decidedly un-feudal way when he told the apostles, "The greatest among you must become like a lesser person, and your leader must be a servant."

Nevertheless, the church adopted the feudal style of government in the latter centuries of the first millennium, holding on to it as it became the almost universal norm in the political order. And whereas civil societies have since moved onto newer forms of governance, the church has chosen to preserve the old ways, shrouding them with quasi-divine approbation.

Whenever priests were accused of abusing minors, bishops instinctively fell back on the first line of defense: "What must we do to protect the system, to keep it intact and stable?" Offending vassals were quickly transferred to other parishes, and just as quickly the whole system of evasion, mental reservation, and secrecy took over.

All the U.S. bishops gathered in Dallas in 2002 and passed a controversial charter to stem the problem. Yet because by then the laypeople were well aware of the hierarchy's arcane system, the bishops were compelled to submit to a review board consisting entirely of laypersons. This violation of a fundamental tenet of feudalism seemed intolerable to some bishops, and a few refused to cooperate. After all, what right had representatives of the lowest echelon to lord it over the lords? Cooler heads argued that resistance on the issue might lead to a massive walkout of the faithful. And after all, the concessions to this lay board would be only a temporary matter. The years have proven that there's nothing temporary about the scandal — not with the occasional flurries of new accusations, not with the millions being paid to victims and lawyers, not with churches being closed and diocesan bankruptcies more than mere speculation, not with the hierarchy determined to resist any talk about "structural reform." The bishops still don't get it.

At some point, I believe, this accumulation of crises will reach a critical mass, and church leadership will have no choice but to get it — as they are carried along by the winds of the Spirit.

Chapter Eleven

Reform from Above

————— ✝ —————

Jesus Christ is best preached as the Savior by a church that is in solidarity with the people whose lives are marked by poverty, oppression, discrimination, and all kinds of injustice. — INDONESIAN BISHOPS CONFERENCE

WHENEVER THE QUESTION of structural change in the church comes up, a common Catholic response is, "No, it won't happen. The people may want it, the challenges of the time may call for it. But 'they' will not allow it."

And who is "they"? The answer is always the same: "the pope, the bishops, the hierarchy; 'they' will never bend."

This attitude, I believe, is responsible in large part for the low morale today among laity and many priests. And certainly, there is plenty of evidence to make a case that the church in the early twenty-first century is resistant to change and, if anything, trying to move the institution backward into some previous century. I was in full agreement with this judgment until I came upon evidence that those at the top are not always and altogether united in maintaining the structure "as it always has been."

A major eye-opener is a 1995 encyclical by Pope John Paul II, which seemed so out of character for the man. It gives a glimpse into his mind and heart shortly before his debilitating illness began to take its toll on his energy and spirit. There is also evidence, I've found, that more than a few of "them" — bishops, archbishops, cardinals — are not straining to hold back the future. They want change for the same reason so many laity want it: that the church may become less closed and centralized, more open to the impulse of the Holy Spirit. In this chapter, we look at three relatively recent instances of participative efforts coming from the church's official leadership.

An Immense Task
"I Cannot Carry Out by Myself"

John Paul's encyclical *Ut Unum Sint* (That All May Be One) is almost a distress signal, prompted by his realization that the ecumenical movement is not really achieving its goals and never will without substantial change at the top of the church. John Quinn, retired archbishop of San Francisco, said the encyclical "is without question a revolutionary document," adding that no other pope has spoken so candidly about his need for assistance.[1]

Vatican II prepared the way for *Ut Unum Sint* when it took a whole new approach to non-Catholic Christians in its Decree on Ecumenism:

> The brethren divided from us also carry out many of the sacred actions of the Christian religion. Undoubtedly ... these actions can truly engender a life of grace and can be rightly described as capable of providing access to the community of salvation.... The Catholic Church accepts them with respect and affection as brothers.... It follows that these separated Churches and Communities ... have by no means been deprived of significance and importance in the mystery of salvation.[2]

For some thirty years these texts led to an unprecedented amount of dialogue involving Catholics, Protestants, and Eastern Orthodox churches. Much has been achieved in terms of defusing old tensions and establishing new common ground on some of the most disputed biblical and theological issues. But out of all this activity, nothing resembling the unity John Paul considered necessary has occurred.

The pope chooses his words carefully, addressing the encyclical to no particular group and referring to himself not as "Holy Father" or "Vicar of Christ" but as "Bishop of Rome" and "Servant of the Servants." He is convinced that the division among Christians is an impediment to the spread of the gospel in the world. "When non-believers meet missionaries who do not agree among themselves, even though they all appeal to Christ, will they be in a position to receive the true message?" he asks.[3] He therefore thinks it "absolutely clear that ecumenism, the movement promoting Christian unity, is not just some sort of 'appendix,' which is added to the Church's traditional activity. Rather ecumenism is an organic part of her life and work, and consequently must pervade all that she is and does."[4] It is equally clear to him that "the ministry of the Bishop of Rome...constitutes a difficulty for most other Christians" and is a continuing hindrance — if not the main hindrance — to ecumenical progress.

He then gets to his major point: "I am convinced that I have a particular responsibility...in acknowledging the ecumenical aspirations of the majority of the Christian Communities and in heeding the request made of me to find a way of exercising the primacy which, while in no way renouncing what is essential to its mission, is nevertheless open to a new situation."[5]

What kind of "new situation"? The implication is that the progress of the ecumenical movement and world events have compelled him to reconsider his proper role in the Christian world. But he is not sure. So he reaches out to "the brethren divided from us," asking for help: "This is an immense task, which we cannot refuse and which I cannot carry out by myself. Could not the real but imperfect communion existing between us persuade Church leaders and their theologians to engage with me in a patient and fraternal dialogue in which, leaving useless controversies behind, we could listen to one another, keeping before us only the will of Christ for his Church?"[6] Here then is Pope John Paul II asking Protestant and Orthodox leaders to assist in redefining the papal office in such a way that it is no longer a stumbling block to reunion. It is interesting that he would open himself to listening and perhaps discovering from non-Catholics the details of the "new situation." It is even more interesting to speculate just what papal baggage he or another pope might be willing to jettison in the interest of bringing Christians together.

Later in the encyclical, John Paul explains he's not prepared to sell the store. There are some essentials that are not open to debate. The mission of the bishop of Rome, he says, is "keeping watch" over the whole church in the service of communion and unity. He lists certain areas of vigilance that have traditionally been connected with the papal primacy, such as vigilance over the church's mission and over the celebration of liturgy and the duty to admonish, caution, and declare at times that certain opinions are destructive of unity. Which sounds at first reading like he's holding onto his position of primacy in the strictest sense.

But then he adds, "All this however must always be done in communion. When the Catholic Church affirms that the office of the Bishop of Rome corresponds to the will of Christ, she does not separate this office from the mission entrusted to the whole body of bishops who are also vicars and ambassadors of Christ. The Bishop of Rome is a member of the 'college,' and the bishops are his brothers in the ministry."[7] In other words, he sees his authority in the new situation as far more collaborative and democratic with respect to the bishops (and leaders of other churches?) than it had been in the past. He even cites the words from the Acts of the Apostles (discussed in the first chapter of this book) when the first followers of Christ met in Jerusalem concerning the requirements of the Mosaic law. "In this new process," says John Paul, "one must not impose any burden beyond that which is strictly necessary."

As it turned out, the message and tone of this encyclical, so different from the pope's authoritative voice in his other writings, did not represent a conversion on his part.

The discussion John Paul sought with the separated brethren did not happen during his tenure, nor did he show any signs of functioning more collegially within his own household of faith in his latter days. But it was at least a momentary stepping down from the throne, a frank admission he did not have the answer to a serious problem and humbly asked for help. There is nothing to prevent his immediate successor, Benedict XVI, or another pontiff from following up on the ecumenical process John Paul spoke of. Benedict did state from his first days that he considers reunion of the Catholic and Orthodox churches a major priority. Nor is there anything to prevent a future pope from reaching out for assistance in solving some other great problem (for instance, the birth control dilemma) that he cannot solve himself. In any event, the *Ut Unum Sint* concept sits, ready for implementation, pointing to a future that most Christians would heartily celebrate.

A New Way of Being Church

When the bishops of Asia returned to their countries after the closing of Vatican II in 1965, they were encouraged by what they had heard. Church in this new era must become sensitive to the cultures, faiths, and ethnic identities of the people it served. The days of "the missionary church," totally dependent on foreign bishops and priests and on Western traditions and policies, had ended; indigenous leadership would mark the future. "The challenge for the Asian leaders was now to find those paths that would allow them to nurture the essence of their faith while separating it from the trappings of the colonial experience," says journalist and author Tom Fox, a longtime student of Asian Catholicism.[8]

The old model of church Asians knew was often referred to as "cookie-cutter" Catholicism, "a one-size-fits-all model . . . using the same language and same rites as Europeans had used for centuries. The condition and needs of local culture simply played no role; they were not to be factored in at all."[9] Many Catholics had grown accustomed to this style of religion and preferred the European model with European saints, statues, and holy cards.

Asian Catholicism was Western Catholicism transplanted to different soil, and it had not flourished. Catholics represent 1 or 2 percent of the population in most Asian countries, and the great distance between Catholic villages and cities left local bishops feeling isolated. Few had an opportunity to work cooperatively with their peers in implementing the ideas of Vatican II. It was said that an Asian bishop was more likely to know a bishop in Rome than one from another Asian country.

However, a kind of epiphany occurred in 1970 when Pope Paul VI visited Manila in the Philippines during a long tour of Asian countries. Virtually all the bishops of South and Southeast Asia gathered for the occasion, the first time many had been together as a single body. Here in the Philippines, whose 32 million Catholics represented almost two-thirds of all Asian Catholics, Paul called for the church to address the justice needs of the countless millions of Asians, to make their human concerns the church's own concerns.

Inspired by this summons, the bishops, under the leadership of men like Cardinals Stephen Kim of South Korea and Valerian Gracias of India, began planning an innovative, collegial approach to their task. Working together, eleven national bishops conferences formed a super-umbrella organization, the Federation of Asian Bishops Conferences, or FABC. Their purpose, they said, was to find "a new way of being church."

Vatican officials of course were opposed to any such body having "binding authority" on moral and doctrinal issues, so Kim assured them the new organization would confine itself to pastoral matters, such as social justice, human development, and communications. This proved to be an advantage in the years to come. Because there was no binding authority, there was more willingness to work in a cooperative spirit.[10]

In the early years the FABC bishops developed a new ecclesiological approach, one that regards promoting and furthering the Kingdom of God as the aim of all activity and ministry. According to Vietnamese theologian Peter Phan, under this policy the church is no longer considered to be the pinnacle or the very center of Christian life. Rather it is removed from the center to the periphery and from the top to the bottom. Like the sun around which the earth and other planets move, the reign of God is the center around which everything in the church revolves and to which everything is subordinated.... The only reason for the church to exist is to serve the reign of God.[11]

Activities that promote the reign, such as peacemaking and forgiveness, feeding the poor, witnessing to justice in oppressive situations, and building responsible families and communities take precedence over making converts or preaching about Jesus. In other words, making the gospel visible comes before talking about it. Only in the context of concrete manifestations of concern, said the bishops, can the life and person of Christ be introduced. After that comes theology and the church.

During their regular plenary assemblies over thirty years, the FABC identified certain characteristics that should mark everything the local church does. Among them:

- A recognition of the fundamental equality of all members of the local church and among the local churches themselves.

- An understanding that all internal church organization is to be participatory and collaborative and never top-down or dictatorial. According to Phan, "In the church loyalty is owed to no one but Christ, and a bishop is not beholden to the pope for his episcopal office nor is he the pope's vicar. It is theologically much more appropriate to describe the relationship between the local church and the pope in terms of collegiality and solidarity."[12]

- A commitment to carrying on an ongoing "three-way dialogue" with Asian cultures, with Asian religions, and with Asian people, especially the poor. "Being a 'small remnant' and likely to remain so for the foreseeable future, Christians must journey with the followers of other Asian religions and together with them — not instead of or, worse, against them — work for the coming of the kingdom of God," says Phan. In this approach, adds Fox, "Catholics were no longer to be viewed as sole possessors of the kingdom, which went well beyond the church."[13]

The new thrust eventually caught the attention of the Vatican. In 1990 Cardinal Joseph Tomko, prefect of the Congregation for the Evangelization of Peoples, arrived from Rome for FABC's fifth plenary assembly. He upbraided the bishops for not making more converts and for failing to make the proclamation of Jesus Christ the church's first priority. From then on Rome exerted pressure on FABC leaders to conform to the New Evangelization announced by Pope John Paul II. The bishops resisted, though the Vatican disapproval has taken a toll on their spirit. So also has the Vatican's practice of replacing retiring Asian bishops with successors who are more conservative or even hostile to this "new way of being church."

In 1998 the Asian bishops were summoned to Rome for a synod with John Paul. As the title of the event, the pope chose "Jesus Christ the Savior and his mission of love and service in Asia that they may have life and have it abundantly." But the bishops held firm to their commitment to their new model of church. The Indonesian delegation said, "Jesus Christ is best preached as the Savior by a church that is in solidarity with the people whose lives are marked by poverty, oppression, discrimination and all kinds of injustice." The Japanese bishops said, "If we stress too much that Jesus Christ is the one and only Savior, we can have no dialogue, common living or solidarity with other religions."[14]

The Japanese delegation also contended that the synod agenda should not be determined by the curia but by the Asian bishops themselves, that the chairpersons be chosen by the Asian bishops and not the curia, and that women and leaders of other Asian religions be invited. During the actual synod sessions, the bishops got little that they wanted, but they did succeed in presenting a united face in defending the value of the triple dialogue. They were also candid in protesting the micromanaging tendencies of Vatican officials, particularly their handling of translations of the liturgical texts. An Indonesian bishop said it makes no sense for bishops' conferences to translate these texts into their local languages, only to then submit them to the Vatican for approval from "people who do not understand our language.... What we need is trust: trust in God and trust in each other."[15]

In his response to the almost two hundred contributions from bishops during the synod, Pope John Paul repeatedly drove home one major point: "Jesus Christ is humanity's one and only Savior." He took no formal action against the FABC approach, but soon after did censure two Catholic theologians, Tissa Balasuriya and Jacques Dupuis, whose vision had helped shape the Asian approach. And less than two years later the pope approved the document *Dominus Iesus* by Cardinal Joseph Ratzinger's Congregation for the Doctrine of the Faith. Through the church alone, it states, the message of Christ comes to all of humanity in a form that is "complete," "definitive," "absolute," "total," "exclusive," "full," and "unique."[16]

Since the synod, the work of the FABC (including fourteen Asian bishops' conferences and eleven auxiliary member conferences) moves steadily ahead through books, documents, seminars, assemblies, and news releases. It is not just the Vatican's lack of approval but the stark economic condition of the continent, the increasing gap between the rich and poor due to globalization, that present the greatest obstacle to further progress at this point.

Their Eyes Were Now Open

In 1976 the U.S. bishops sponsored the Call to Action Conference, an unprecedented experiment in participatory democracy. Conceived, developed, and delivered under the hierarchy's auspices, the event was intended as the church's contribution to the nation's bicentennial celebration. Detroit Cardinal John Dearden envisioned the conference as a first step toward a decentralized U.S. church. For three days in October, it occupied the complete attention of 1,351 delegates and some 1,500 observers in Detroit's cavernous Cobo Hall. They did not come unprepared. Over a two-year period, the organizers had distilled the suggestions and recommendations of some 800,000 Catholics, who presented their candid views at parishes and during a series of regional hearings all over the country. The overriding question was, where should the American Catholic Church place its priorities for the next hundred years?

The process was a breakthrough, says theologian Dennis McCann, "for it indissolubly wed traditional Catholic social teaching, heretofore concerned with substantive issues in society … with the spirit of collegiality emanating from Vatican II."[17]

You will find scant mention of this historic occasion in Catholic accounts of the post–Vatican II era. This Call to Action, like some earlier movements in church history discussed in this book, has been buried and mostly forgotten by the institutional leadership, almost as if it never happened. It survives in only one living and vital offspring, which continues to bear witness to the experiment, though unacknowledged by its parent bishops. Its work will be discussed in the next chapter.

In the fall of 1976 hopes were high. The bishops wanted these people — laity, priests, sisters — to speak their minds openly, candidly. What thoughts and proposals did they have for the church in the next hundred years? The extraordinarily detailed process virtually ruled out the likelihood of acrimonious debate, protracted bickering, or filibusters. This was a good old American town hall meeting using Robert's tried-and-true Rules of Order, only on a more ambitious, grander scale. Early on in the sessions, some clerics saw what was happening and despaired. Archbishop Bernard Law reportedly cornered Monsignor Jack Egan, co-chair of the proceedings, and said, "Jack, we have to adjourn this meeting right now." Egan replied, "The people have a right to express their minds.... You go back and sit down."[18]

When the work was completed, the votes were tallied on some 180 issues, and the gavel banged for the last time. Here are some of the more salient resolutions passed by the assembly.

- If the church is to teach credibly about social justice and human rights, it must apply these teachings to its own internal life.

- Pastors must be open and accountable to parishioners, especially on financial matters.

- The bishops' conference should petition the pope to allow married men to be ordained to the priesthood.

- The bishops should create a "more developed position" on the ordination of women.

- The response of the Catholic community to church teaching on race and ethnicity — a "mockery" in most places — demands immediate attention and action.

- Church leadership should be committed to the right of diverse ethnic, racial, and cultural groups to develop their distinctive customs and traditions, including language.

- Church leaders should publicly address the request of the divorced who have remarried to receive, under certain conditions, the sacraments of the church.

- Consideration should be given to allowing unordained men, married couples, and laicized priests to preach and give homilies at Mass.

- The church must root out those structures and attitudes which discriminate against homosexuals as persons.

- The American bishops should use their pastoral leadership to affirm more clearly the right and responsibility of married people to form their own consciences and to discern what is appropriate within the context of their own marriage.

- The church should support amnesty for undocumented immigrants whose departure would impose hardship.

- The U.S. Catholic community should condemn and be among those who resist the production, possession, proliferation, and threatened use of nuclear weapons, even in a policy of deterrence.

The delegates left in a state of euphoria, confident that they had set the church on a progressive course. All the recommendations, they were assured, would be taken up by the bishops' conference at its next meeting some six months away, and they would be evaluated, tested, and, to a great extent, implemented over a five-year period. To be sure, all the recommendations were not as edgy as the ones cited above; some were simply calls for church leaders to do a better job of what they were already doing. The ones above were not on the preparatory documents studied by all the participants nor on the agenda; no one anticipated they would arise. So the average delegate was scarcely aware of the state of shock gripping many of the bishops present, including some who had guided the process from the beginning. "What happened?" they asked. "Were we mugged?"

One explanation was that the conference had been kidnapped by a gang of liberals and special-agenda elitists who manipulated the other delegates into siding with their leftist views. But that explanation had no merit. Ninety-three percent of the delegates were persons appointed by the bishops or bishops themselves. A third were priests, most of them associated with diocesan offices. Seven percent were representing national organizations, most of them centrist or right of center, like the National Council of Catholic Women or Catholics United for the Faith. According to some observers, a shift occurred when the delegates were broken up into small groups of seven or eight. Here, says McCann,

> they began to shape their segment of the action recommendations into the advice they wished to set forth. Continuity there would be with the previous documents but the emerging documents would be their own. . . . The dynamics of the process . . . stimulated an expansion of consciousness that could not help but judge the church's own practices by

the same standard they were being encouraged to use to judge other institutions of society.... The credibility of the church's critical participation in the affairs of the world inescapably depends upon the quality of critical participation allowed in the church itself. The delegates had tasted the fruit of collegiality and their eyes were now open.[19]

Cardinal Dearden, the principal architect of the Call to Action Conference, did not appear alarmed in his report to the bishops two weeks after the event:

The results of the bicentennial process may at this point seem hasty, untidy, careless, even extreme. But...it seems to me...the working papers and conference resolutions demonstrate a warmth and sympathy for the problems of Church leadership on the part of our people,...their sincere willingness to share in building a stronger Church, and their firm resolve to fulfill a Christian ministry in the world. No one expects us to endorse all that transpired in Detroit. People do expect us to continue the process.[20]

But many other members of the hierarchy feared any follow-up would open a Pandora's box of controversial issues. They heard what the people wanted and did not like it. At the bishop's meeting the next May, Archbishop Joseph Bernardin, president of the bishops' conference, reportedly said the delegates "tried to do too much." He appointed a task force to review and follow up on the recommendations. No conference participants were named to the group, nor were Dearden and Archbishop Peter Gerety, major supporters of the event and its recommendations. Instead, the task force was composed mainly of bishops opposed to the idea from the beginning. Needless to say, the whole effort was tabled and the follow-up never happened. A few dioceses attempted to have discussions on the Call to Action Conference, but these were strictly pro forma and disintegrated under the pressure of new business.

Historian David O'Brien, who was intimately involved in the conference process, said, "The bishops in effect turned away from the process and the product." Yet, he insisted, "The process worked. People across a wide span of differences listened to one another and shared responsibility. But the bishops did not carry through." And that, he regards, as a supreme disappointment.[21]

At bottom, it seems, the operation worked but the patient died of neglect. What needs to be carefully remembered is that an ambitious national democratic process was carried out with all levels of the church, including many bishops, working in cooperation. The old myth about the people not caring was dispelled in this case. The lessons learned in Detroit, and afterward, could be extremely helpful — the next time.

Chapter Twelve

Pressure from Below

———— ✝ ————

With lay people involved in the decision making, certainly no priest who had abused a child would have been transferred to another parish and allowed to molest other children — parents would never have permitted it.
— JAMES MULLER

JUST TWO YEARS AFTER the Detroit Call to Action Conference, I attended the first meeting of the Chicago Call to Action organization. It was held in a Catholic girls high school near my home, and I walked over. Present, as I recall, were about seventy or eighty, many of whom I recognized as the old Catholic Action activists who had made the Chicago archdiocese a vibrant center of progressive ideas in the 1940s and 1950s. There was Patty Crowley, who, with her now deceased husband, Pat, had spread the Christian Family Movement all over the world; and there was Monsignor Jack Egan, a tireless advocate for social justice in the city and nation; and John McDermott, a loud voice for racial equality in Chicago; and Ed Marciniak, who could recite the papal social encyclicals almost by heart; and Russ Barta, who ran a network of adult education centers on theology and the role of the laity years before Vatican II.

They were there at the invitation of Dan Daley, a former Chicago priest with a degree in urban studies. Always fascinated with the story of American democracy and its implications for the church, Daley thought the Detroit recommendations ought to be resurrected — and if not here, where? He proposed the launch of a Chicago organization that would press for many of the justice issues that came out of the conference only to quickly disappear from the church's radar: issues like women priests, reconciliation for divorced and remarried couples, optional celibacy for priests, and financial openness in the church. Chicago seemed an especially apt stage for such an organization, since the archbishop, Cardinal John Cody, had offended just about everyone in the local church with his autocratic antics and arrogant mishandling of church funds. This new Call to Action, known forever after as "CTA," would become Chicago's progressive church voice and watchdog of the institution.

Yet as I looked around the room, I doubted that anything substantial could come of this. The veteran activists were mostly in their sixties and seventies. They could hardly be counted on for the heavy lifting. In my mid-forties at the time, I was among the junior participants. Would Catholics care enough about church reform to get involved in this dispirited archdiocese? True, there was a lot of energy and lively conversation at this meeting, but I had to wonder if this was less a birth than a jovial Irish wake for the old guard.

Eighteen years later when there was near gridlock in the packed corridors outside the workshops in Detroit's Cobo Hall, I thought about that first meeting. This was the seventeenth annual gathering of the new CTA with more than five thousand people in attendance. Most looked like the old folks at that first meeting in the high school. But — except for ageless Patty Crowley, Jack Egan, and a handful of others — they were not the same senior citizens. They were people from virtually every state and a few foreign countries who had gravitated to CTA over the years. And here in 1996, there was a notable representation of middle-aged and younger people too, commemorating that original Call to Action Conference whose spirit hadn't died after all.

In fact, the years since 1978 have seen the rising of scores of church-reform groups, some with very specific agendas, some with broad plans, some taking on the institutional church directly and aggressively, some seeking a more diplomatic route through persuasion and dialogue, some changing their approach as time passes. I think it would be fair to say that all, regardless of the path taken, have met resistance from church leadership and all, including Call to Action, have been tested in the fire. None of course has caught the eye of the public as much as the Voice of the Faithful, which in 2002 grew from a handful of parishioners in a church basement in Boston to a national movement within three months. The pressure for greater openness and participation exerted by these organizations triggers an almost knee-jerk reaction in the hierarchy because it strikes at its insistence on exclusive, unyielding power — an area where the hierarchy's claims are weakest. The Grand Inquisitor would surely understand this and deal swiftly with those who presume to challenge.

CTA — A Call for Consultation

In its first years the Chicago Call to Action presented itself as "rooted in church teaching," but as the institutional church, under Pope John Paul II, drifted farther and farther to the right, CTA came to be seen as liberal and dissenting. The original dissent was mainly over Cardinal Cody's arbitrary, secretive policies. In its yearly conferences and publications (which my wife, Margaret, and I edited for ten years), it presented documentation and cried out for fiscal responsibility and transparency. It also called for a more effective lay voice in parish councils and improved benefits for Catholic school teachers. Under the codirectorship of Dan Daley and his wife, Sheila, the CTA staff, board, and membership became involved in societal issues like the nuclear disarmament movement, opposition to U.S. interference in Latin America, and a national campaign to gather clothing for the poor in Nicaragua. The organization in the 1980s sponsored a group of young actors who created musicals based on the U.S. bishops' pastoral letters on peace and the economy. Membership grew slowly and steadily, but the yearly conferences rarely drew more than four hundred, except when a luminary like Hans Küng spoke and attendance spiked at eighteen hundred.

In 1990 the Daleys and the CTA board ran a full-page ad in the *New York Times,* urging readers to sign a "Call for Reform" statement. Among the calls and appeals in the letter (which still constitute CTA's basic platform):

- We call upon the church to discard the medieval discipline of mandatory priestly celibacy and open the priesthood to women and married men.

- We call for extensive consultation with the Catholic people in developing church teaching on human sexuality.

- We claim our responsibility as committed laity, religious, and clergy, to participate in the selection of our local bishops.

- We call for open dialogue, academic freedom, and due process.

- We appeal to the institutional church to reform and renew its structures. We also appeal to the people of God to witness to the Spirit who lives within us and to seek ways to serve the vision of God in human society.

The document quickly gained twenty-five thousand signers and several thousand new paid members. The yearly conferences, featuring speakers like Sister Joan Chittister, Edwina Gately, Richard McBrien, and Charles Curran, began to draw upward of three thousand, and membership rose to more than twenty thousand. In 1996 Bishop Fabian Bruskewitz's out-of-the-blue excommunication of CTA members in his Lincoln, Nebraska, diocese, without a hearing or offer of evidence, also promoted a membership boom, raising the total to more than twenty-five thousand.

With Cardinal Cody's death in 1982 and the arrival of Joseph Bernardin as archbishop of Chicago, CTA had less to complain about in the local church. He took no direct action against the group but gave it no encouragement. Only in his latter days did Bernardin meet cordially with CTA leadership. On one occasion he acknowledged he was beginning to have second thoughts about the ban on women's ordination. His successor, Cardinal Francis George, had no such misgivings and made it quite clear he had no respect for liberally inclined movements.

I was present when in 1998 George told a gathering of the National Center of the Laity that "liberal Catholicism is an exhausted project" and "parasitical on a substance that no longer exists." It lacks the ability to pass on the faith "in its integrity," he explained, suggesting the proper alternative is "simply Catholicism." Other bishops have been more aggressive, banning CTA meetings on church property or publicly condemning the organization for fostering dissent. In 2006 the archbishop of Milwaukee wrote to many of the speakers who were scheduled for the CTA conference in that city urging them to cancel their appearance. Only one did.

Leaders and staff have been helping local members establish some forty regional CTA chapters around the country, many becoming active in their own local dioceses concerning societal justice issues and sponsoring, in some cases, their own area or state CTA conferences. The Syracuse, New York, chapter launched a survey that revealed that active priests nationally favor optional celibacy. And a chapter in rural Belleville, Illinois, pioneered the concept of "lay Catholic synods," opportunities for ordinary Catholics to make known their vision of the church to come. The synod approach has become popular in other dioceses. In recent years the national CTA organization introduced two new thrusts: an exhaustive anti-racism program and the "Just Church" project which aims to put a spotlight on those areas in the country where hierarchical power is allegedly perpetrating singular abuses. News of its activities is disseminated through CTA's three regular publications, a detailed website, and frequent news releases to the secular press.

VOTF —
Rooting Out the Pathology

It began in early 2002 as a discussion group in a Boston parish. The revelations about local priests abusing children and the cover-ups of these crimes by the local hierarchy appearing daily in the *Boston Globe* convinced Dr. James Muller, a member of the parish, that ordinary laypeople needed to air their reactions. Muller, a co-founder of the Nobel Prize–winning group International Physicians for the Prevention of Nuclear War, is a man who knows a bit about organizing, and soon the Monday evening meetings of an organization, soon to be called Voice of the Faithful (VOTF), were drawing two hundred or more persons to a church basement. Some came to tell stories of their own abuse, others to talk of a child or relative who had suffered abuse and to relate amid tears that the church did nothing about it. Many came to express their outrage or just to confirm what seemed unbelievable. There was a growing general consensus that this time the church had to do something, and these people saw themselves as the church.

As the allegations in the *Globe* grew more numerous and the church's failure to act grew more apparent, television networks, newspapers, and magazines began to take notice. Similar reports against priests and bishops elsewhere were making headlines all over the country. This wasn't just a local story; it was an epidemic. The intense, growing group in Boston provided the press with a perfect microcosm of the reaction.

Muller and two other members scheduled a meeting with a Boston auxiliary bishop. On the day of the meeting, Muller recalled, "we wanted to be embraced by the hierarchy, to work in partnership with them. Our goal was to forge a trusting relationship with [Cardinal Bernard Law] and others in the hierarchy so that the laity could gain a seat at the table, become part of the process of decision making and build a better church."

The VOTF delegation was quickly relieved of its naivete. They learned that the bishop, under orders from Law, had already been calling Boston pastors, telling them to prohibit VOTF members from meeting on church property. His organization now realized, said Muller, that "the scandal was a symptom of the underlying problem of unbalanced power in the hands of fallible humans — a flawed structure that had led to the cover-up and many other problems" in the twentieth century.[1]

Soon thousands of people were checking VOTF's website and signing up to endorse its three goals — to support survivors of clergy sexual abuse, to support priests of integrity, and to shape structural change to ensure that such problems do not recur. Some were eagerly forming their own local affiliates. The goals seemed so innocent and straightforward, but VOTF would discover that the very mention of those two words, "structural change," would cause instant panic in many a clerical mind.

In March Cardinal Law called together some three thousand lay leaders, but he was less than apologetic, telling them to trust him and his staff to solve the problem. A month later the VOTF organization, after painful discernment, publicly called for his resignation. So did the *Boston Globe*. Law traveled to Rome and reportedly offered to step down, but the pope advised him to stay the course. As summer approached, VOTF was no longer a lobbying organization but a major power with committees, projects, and ready responses to the flood of media inquiries. When parish contributions dropped precipitously in the archdiocese, VOTF developed the Voice of Compassion project. People who were no longer willing to give directly to the church could give instead to VOTF, which guaranteed the money would go for needy Catholic services. The effort was successful, though Law condemned it and forbade Catholic Charities from accepting the $56,000 that was gathered. Another project, to band the Boston parish councils together for communication purposes and "to curb the culture of insularity and secrecy within the hierarchy" was also vetoed by church officials. Commented David Zwick, a VOTF leader, "There is a pathology in our church that needs to be rooted out, and people are going to begin voting with their feet if we don't do something about it."[2]

Much labor went into preparing for the first Response of the Faithful convention to be held in July. Muller told the *Globe* of his dream that in three years half the Catholic world would be enrolled in VOTF and that every parish, every diocese, and every nation would have a chapter. At the same time he worried that only a handful would show up for the convention. The whole thing was growing so fast, it could easily get out of control. He wanted the public to understand that he and the other leaders were only interested in helping, not in overthrowing authority. Talk of structural reform, he reiterated, was exclusively related to governance of the church, not to doctrine. His major fear was alleviated when some forty-two hundred people showed up in July at the huge convention center.

Speaker Tom Doyle, a priest who warned the U.S. bishops in vain years before that they had a ticking time bomb on their hands with the abuse situation, provided a barnburner of a speech:

> What we see happening around us are the initial death throes of the medieval monarchical model of the church. This was an institutional church that was based on the belief that small, select minority of the educated, the privileged and the powerful was called by Almighty God to manage the temporal and spiritual lives of the faceless masses, on the presumption that their unlettered and squalid state meant that they were ignorant and incapable of discerning their spiritual destiny. This is 2002 and not 1302, and that model is based on a myth that is long dead, if in fact it was ever remotely grounded in a sliver of reality.[3]

Attorney Jim Post offered the image of a very big table that could accommodate a diverse range of the faithful — survivors and their parents and siblings, "women religious whose voices have too often not been heard, priests, men and women who have been away from the church, people who celebrate Vatican II and people who want to celebrate the Latin mass."[4]

Others appeared to tone down the more ecstatic deliveries. Said theologian Lisa Sowle Cahill, "Even though we are beginning new reforms . . . right here at this convention, we also need not to become too directly oppositional to the official structure. The pope and the bishops are also part of historic Catholicism, and if we are too confrontational . . . we might become labeled as fringe types and outsiders."[5]

At the end Muller was satisfied. "As a movement, Voice of the Faithful emerged from the convention significantly empowered," he later wrote, "with positive worldwide publicity. We have been established as a force to be reckoned with. In just a few short months our movement had grown from a gathering in a church basement to a force for democracy within the Roman Catholic Church."[6]

The message was not received well by Cardinal Law. Although he at first barred VOTF from using church property, he soon modified the ruling. Some other bishops in the East and throughout the country also declared the organization unwelcome on their property. So despite its efforts to maintain an orthodox posture, VOTF was labeled an outsider nevertheless. When Muller and other leaders finally met with Law in November, the cardinal remained angry and unapologetic as ever. But a letter from fifty-eight Boston priests urging the cardinal to resign apparently did shake him. "The priests and people of Boston have lost confidence in you as their spiritual director," they wrote.[7] Almost simultaneously, some ten thousand pages of archdiocesan personnel records revealing a pattern of gross concealment were released. And in early December Law finally submitted his resignation to the pope. There was little doubt anywhere that the infant organization had played a major part in Law's departure.

After that first spectacular year, the publicity died down, and there have been considerable shifts in top leadership. The organization, with some thirty-five thousand signer-members, has moved in a variety of new directions: sponsoring a national petition urging the bishops' conference to fund and complete a study to determine "the underlying structural and cultural causes of the abuse scandal"; working to overturn the statute of limitations in many states, thus allowing the prosecution of guilty clergy; and aiding some 150 VOTF affiliates in the United States with their own local agendas.

It is tempting to compare CTA, the old veteran of the reform movement, with VOTF, the charismatic new kid on the block. In fact, a great many active Catholics are members of both groups, and leaders of both are in regular contact. The most obvious difference is in CTA's call for change in church governance and its insistence that certain doctrines, the ban on women priests, for example, must also be re-evaluated and changed. CTA can therefore be regarded as in disagreement with authoritative church doctrine. On the other hand, VOTF is on record as seeking changes only in church governance. Thus, it could campaign for optional celibacy in the priesthood and a vast increase of lay participation in diocesan and parish decision making. But by its own self-definition, it cannot criticize current teaching on women priests, birth control, divorce and remarriage, in vitro fertilization, homosexuality, stem cell research, or a dozen other matters that the hierarchical church regards as doctrinal. As a longtime member of Call to Action, I think that governance and doctrine cannot be forever separated if lasting reform is to happen. I also believe the hierarchy thinks so too, and that is one reason why VOTF's goal of "structural reform" is so upsetting that church leaders like Cardinal Law sought to stifle the organization even in its earliest stages. There is fear that if the boat is rocked just a little bit, it might capsize.

A Universe of Reformers

In the vast universe of liberal reform groups, many are guided by powerful, outspoken leaders who use their skills to analyze, inform, lobby, and inspire. One such leader is Christine Schenk, a sister of St. Joseph and co-founder of the Cleveland-based, five-thousand-member FutureChurch organization. She is a constant creator of ideas and strategies for the movement. FutureChurch came into being in 1990 when a Cleveland-area parish passed a resolution calling on the U.S. bishops to consider opening the priesthood to women and to married persons of either sex. Some thirty other parishes supported the initiative, and the organization that grew out of one parish's resolution has become a national network of parish-based activists. Schenk, a former organizer for the United Farm Workers union, and her staff work closely with Call to Action, and the two are frequently partnered in plans and projects.

In 1995 FutureChurch created a Future of Priestly Ministry project, which digested tons of data, articles, and information about the priest shortage into parishioner-friendly, compact folders. The purpose was to awaken Catholics to the seriousness of the problem, to get them discussing its causes and implications, and to stimulate strategizing about what they can do, as laity, to address the issues. Hundreds of these packets have gone out to interested parishes, along with tips on media relations, community organizing, and contacting church officials regarding their determination to keep the Eucharist alive in their area.

Even more noteworthy has been the Women in Church Leadership project, which profiled strong women Catholic leaders like Catherine of Siena, Hildegard of Bingen, Dorothy Day, and Mary Magdalene in folder form. Schenk made a special effort to call public attention to "the real" Mary Magdalene, not a prostitute but a close disciple of Jesus and the first person to whom he appeared after his resurrection. FutureChurch designed a liturgical service in her honor that could be celebrated in any parish setting. The idea caught on, and parishes nationwide began holding the service yearly. When the fictional novel *The Da Vinci Code* became an ongoing phenomenon, the media took notice of Schenk's work. Stories of the church services in honor of Mary Magdalene, "the apostle to the apostles" and strong woman leader, appeared in *Time, Newsweek,* and major newspapers and on television news in scores of cities. Every year the number of parishes celebrating her has grown, and the devotion has spread to foreign countries.

Meanwhile, FutureChurch ideas, new projects, and up-to-date commentary on every newsworthy development in Catholicism appear on the organization's website.

Another powerful reform voice is Anthony Padovano, a married priest who has been at the center of the CORPUS organization since its founding in 1974. Originally an association for priests who had left canonical ministry, CORPUS now describes itself as "a ministerial faith community, rooted in a strong Eucharistic commitment, promoting an expanded and renewed priesthood of married and single men and women in the Catholic Church." The organization is home to many formerly canonical priests who believe sacramental ministry is not incompatible with marriage, some of whom continue to function in priestly roles as chaplains and as presiders at weddings, funerals, and other liturgical events when requested. Some also serve as pastors of unofficial Catholic churches, saying Mass and providing a full sacramental ministry.

Padovano, who is in touch with most other reform groups, including the European WE ARE CHURCH organization, provides in his writings and talks an optimistic view of a reformed and renewed Catholicism. Speaking at the 2006 CORPUS conference in Pittsburgh, he regarded the changes in Catholicism over the last half-century as steps in a Spirit-sanctioned evolutionary process:

> In a sense the church told us in Vatican II to see it as a less total reality than we once thought it was. Its document on the modern world, its instruction on ecumenism and world religions, its declaration on conscience and religious freedom taught the truth of God was in other religious institutions (none of which are Catholic) and in our own consciences (even when the church did not officially approve). Once we grasped this, we would never again be what we once were.[8]

Ruth Fitzpatrick is a veteran activist who led the Women's Ordination Conference (WOC) for many years. WOC traces its origin to a woman named Mary Lynch, who wrote on her 1974 Christmas cards, "Isn't it time that women become priests?" Thirty-one of her women friends and one man replied yes. The word spread, and in 1975 some nineteen hundred women gathered in Detroit for the first WOC conference. Under Fitzpatrick's leadership, the group coordinated protests at major cathedrals in the United States, held hearings on women in church and society, and raised for many women (and men) the issue of women in the priesthood for the first time. A WOC delegation descended on the bishops' conference in the early 1980s and insisted on the necessity of an ongoing dialogue. For three years WOC members did meet regularly with the bishops' Committee on Women in the Church, but no real progress was achieved, largely due to Pope John Paul's repeated insistence during those years that the church has no authority to ordain women. It was with the support and under the inspiration of WOC that Sister Theresa Kane, president of the Leadership Conference of Women Religious, publicly urged John Paul during his visit to the United States in 1979 to "permit women to serve in all the ministries of the Catholic Church."

Fitzpatrick and other WOC leaders strove mightily to aid the bishops in their effort to formulate a meaningful pastoral letter on women in the church, but the project was discarded when the Vatican disagreed with the tone of the draft. As perhaps the most visible voice for women priests in the church, WOC has stayed on message with workshops, retreats, and special strategies such as its Take-a-Bishop-to-Breakfast project and its campaign to have women included in the footwashing ceremony during the Holy Thursday liturgies.

Leonard Swidler has headed the Association for the Rights of Catholics in the Church (ARCC) since it was formed in 1980. It is primarily a think tank, publishing documents and holding seminars on legal rights and responsibilities of Catholics and interacting with canon lawyers and other Catholic academics. Under Swidler, ARCC is tireless in promoting the idea of formal constitutions for every level of the church as a curb against arbitrary clerical power. One such constitution declares all members of the faith have, among other things, the right to a voice in decisions that affect them, the right to follow their informed conscience, and the right to express publicly their agreement or disagreement regarding decisions made by church members. It also states that members of all councils in the church shall be elected and operate in a democratic, one-person-one-vote manner.

Women Priests — Action in a Transitional Time

For more than thirty years Catholic women have been expressing a call to priesthood, and more than a few have left the church to pursue their vocation in Protestant churches. Within the church the call remains persistent, giving birth to a veritable armada of national and international groups pressing for ordination. Besides WOC, there's WOW (Women's Ordination Worldwide), Women-Church Convergence, and Roman Catholic WomenPriests, to name some of the better known. And the push has escalated to a new level in the new millennium. Where male reformers have feared to tread in terms of confronting the magisterium, women have dared to go. And they are going in increasing numbers. Since 2002 there has been a series of ordinations of women as priests and deacons and the consecrations of some women as bishops, both in Europe and the United States. From the start, the ordaining clergy have been validly ordained Catholic bishops, most of them from bodies like the Polish National Catholic Church and the Old Catholic Church, which are considered by the Vatican as separated from the Roman Church and in a state of schism. In at least one case an ordaining bishop was reportedly an active Roman Catholic serving in an American diocese.

Needless to say, the organizers of these rites are careful about identifying the presiding bishops and the women who receive ordination. In the eyes of the Vatican, these ceremonies are neither licit nor valid, since, as the Congregation for the Doctrine of the Faith has ruled, women lack a "resemblance" to Christ. The first group, seven women ordained on a boat in the Danube River on the border of Germany in 2002, were declared excommunicated by the Vatican, but the Vatican has been less explicit since. Several of these ordinations have occurred in the United States, and many more are expected. It is not clear what organization or combination of organizations is behind all this activity occurring in scattered places around the world, and the lack of clarity is apparently deliberate. Currently, Roman Catholic WomenPriests is a major source of information and coordination.

The most public voice for the phenomenon is Patricia Fresen, who was ordained a priest and later consecrated a bishop in Spain in 2003. A native of South Africa and a Dominican sister for forty-five years, she studied theology in Rome and taught systematic theology, homiletics, and spirituality in a major South African seminary for seven years before deciding to follow a call to the priesthood. She is in charge of coordinating the preparation program for the women candidates and said it is quite demanding in terms of requiring theological and pastoral skills.

In a 2005 talk to members of WOC in Pittsburgh, Fresen said Catholic women are taking this step now out of "prophetic obedience," which involves a changed understanding of authority and obedience:

> The role of leadership is not to give orders but to call the community to be about what they have said they are about — challenging them to be who they are. Prophetic obedience leads us towards the recognition of equality, discipleship of equals, rather than the older family model (father, mother — superior, subject) still often found in the church. ... We are moving from this older model towards co-authority, co-obedience and interdependence.

Not all reform advocates approve the trend toward these ordinations. They see it as buying into an oppressive, outmoded
system, which needs to be renewed at its root, and they fear
women will be co-opted into the dying clerical culture. To this
Fresen replied, "Because we are in a transitional time we need to
claim for women their equal right with men to be ordained. And
we need to do this *contra legem* [against the law], to break an
unjust law and yet to remain firmly within the church....If in
this transitional stage we do not ordain women but merely bless
the ministries of everyone, we will do nothing toward claiming
equal rights for women in the church. And I believe that no one
would take us seriously."[9]

Meanwhile, a new umbrella organization, the Women's Justice Coalition, is attempting to bring a measure of coordination
to all the women reform bodies, most of which approve women's
ordination but are not themselves moving in that direction. According to Rea Howarth, coalition coordinator, the aim is to
get the groups together for at least one shared project a year.
Howarth, who is associated with the Quixote Center in Washington, D.C., observed that the new women priests and bishops
are much in demand for providing the sacrament of reconciliation and as presiders at funerals and weddings, although they
must be discreet about their ministry, since many are employed
by the Catholic Church and would be instantly fired if their activities were made public. "None of us knows where all this is
going," she said. "If the fruits are good, if it's beneficial for the
people of God, then at some point the institutional church is
going to have to deal with it. The truth will prevail."[10]

Is Anybody Listening?

So how much good has come from all the conferences, the pick-
eting, the press releases, the seminars, the mailings, the energy
expended by all these Catholic reform groups? From my own experience with Call to Action, I can cite at least three significant

achievements. First, the movement has educated a lot of Catholics about theology and liturgy and spirituality. It has stirred them to re-examine old assumptions and think about their faith in new ways and to pray in new ways. It has inspired people, who had never seriously thought about these things before to become involved in social justice in the world and in the church.

Second, it has raised the consciousness of Catholics who are not involved in reform action, including the many who don't practice their religion regularly and those fully satisfied with the church as it is. They know something is astir, that there is more than one way of thinking about Catholicism.

Third, the reform organizations have kept many people in the church who would otherwise be gone. You cannot attend a CTA national conference or a meeting of VOTF or CORPUS or NOW without hearing the comments:

- "I come here once a year for nourishment because the parish at home is dead."
- "This where I see life and hope for the future."
- "I had given up and thought all Catholics were the same until I started listening."
- "We have to take action; we can't just sit and wait."

Since 1991 Bill Thompson has been the convener of COR (Catholic Organizations for Renewal). Its sole purpose is to bring together as many reform groups as possible twice a year to discuss their activities and share their plans. Thompson is convinced the movement has been a major factor in preparing the ground for something new. Like Howarth, he is not sure how it will come about but is certain the authoritarian style will not survive. He cites the VOTF experience as evidence.

Thompson, who lives in Boston and is publications director for CTA, noted that Boston Catholics had no previous history of activism or dissatisfaction with the church. "They pretty much accepted the top-down model and lived with a clerical-centered understanding," he said. "Nobody felt moved to do anything.

But when you look at the speed and breadth of their response to the betrayal, the lightning-like growth of VOTF, you see that they were ready." Some of this can be attributed to the fact that for at least two generations the concepts of Vatican II have been taught and discussed in Catholic institutions like Boston College, said Thompson, so the idea of laity rising up and taking control of their church had been fermenting for a long time. "This has changed everything!" he said, referring to Catholics in Boston and all over the country. "The people are never going back to passive acceptance of what Father says or what the bishop says. It's just not going to happen!"[11]

Part III

THE FUTURE

Chapter 13

The Vision Presses On
to Fulfillment

$$\text{\textdagger}$$

*Ultimately pragmatic, the organization will eventually and
inevitably make peace with its own people.*

— EUGENE KENNEDY

T HE ESSENTIAL ARGUMENT of this book is that the community
Jesus established lost one of its basic characteristics along
the way. In its earliest phase it strove to be one, holy, catholic,
apostolic, and participative. Gradually, that participative function was subsumed by a top-down, monarchical element. Jesus
himself had been quite explicit that leadership must not "lord it
over" members of the community. The reign of God, which he
proclaimed, would operate in a completely different fashion: the
first would be last, the leader would be the servant of all, and
the poor would be favored over the rich. That participative energy could not be totally smothered even as the church over the
centuries imitated the top-down governance style of the Roman
Empire and medieval feudalism. Participation was preserved in
the third century by Cyprian of Carthage, for example, who insisted that the people vote on important decisions. It expressed
itself vehemently in the fourth century in the laity's refusal to
accept the hierarchy's nearly unanimous surrender to the Arian
heresy. In the sixth century it showed itself in Gregory the Great's
collaborative style of leadership. The abiding conviction that the
Holy Spirit operated in the whole church gave rise in the eleventh

century to notions of community and individual rights, constitutional guarantees, the people's consent, and representative government — concepts eventually enshrined by civil governments, though not by the church from which they originated. The push for participation was in view in the mighty struggle at the Council of Constance in the fifteenth century, in the effort to construct a distinctively American church in the eighteenth century — and in scores of other historical movements, incidents, and experiments. But the time was not right.

Now in the twenty-first century, I contend, the time is right for the recovery of that full, open, communal participation long under shadow. So much has changed. The rise of the laity, the widespread acceptance of democracy, the developments in theological and biblical interpretation, the emphasis on the church as the People of God, the ideal of collegial decision making, the whole thrust of the Second Vatican Council, ironically even the sense of crisis and uncertainty — all set the stage for a momentous future.

The natural reaction to such a statement is, how could this possibly happen? In the church now, right and left, conservative and liberal, are at each other's throats, the Vatican is apparently steering the ship backward, episcopal leadership has never been more lacking in nerve and creativity, modern culture is hopelessly hedonistic, and the world situation is frighteningly unstable.

Exactly! Christianity is a religion of paradox and surprises. Jesus' parables turn logic on its head. So does his life, death, and resurrection, and so does the history of Christianity. The sin of the Grand Inquisitor was not the lust for power. It was the sin against hope, the sin of all those powerful leaders down through history who trusted too much in themselves, in their logic and their ability to control.

How could recovery happen? It might come with the stroke of a pen by an audacious future pope. It might come through one of the scenarios suggested in this chapter or through a combination of several scenarios or through a completely unexpected event or series of events. However it comes, it will not come without opposition, complaints, and struggle. It may take a long time, or it could happen sooner than anyone expects. It will happen; the process is already under way.

Moving from Consultative to Deliberative

Scenario 1: The machinery is in place for a democratized Catholic Church anywhere in the world. The Second Vatican Council called for regular synods, that is, open meetings and discussions between the pope and bishops. It strongly recommended national or multinational regional conferences of bishops. It found it "highly desirable" that each diocese have a pastoral council in place, with participation by the bishop and clergy and lay members. In the aftermath of Vatican II, canon law provided for parish councils, including the pastors and lay representatives of the parish body, and for parish finance councils to oversee the appropriate use of parish funds. All these bodies are theoretically collaborative and collegial in character and are considered commonplace today in institutional Catholicism. Modeled on democratic principles, they are forums suitable for sorting through relevant issues, proceeding to debate and discussion, and finally resulting in decision by majority vote or some form of consensus.

But these church bodies are de facto peculiarly undemocratic because, under present church law, they are consultative or advisory only, not deliberative or decision-making. Each level of authority, pope, bishop, pastor, is free to heed or not heed the decisions of any synod, senate, or council. As set forth plainly in canon law, these collaborative groups are universally impotent; clerics have the final word. Advisory bodies are like brand-new automobiles with supercharged, eight-cylinder engines, magnetic ride control, power retractable roof, and Corinthian leather seats — but lay drivers have no gas. Only the leaders have access. This could change overnight by expunging a word or two in canons 514 and 536, making some of these groups decision-making entities. Other changes would follow quite quickly.

Meanwhile something is happening to the system at the grass roots. There are pastors and their congregations (and some bishops) who have quietly chosen to regard these consultative entities *as if* they were deliberative, to treat them as having decision-making authority, to honor their decisions as the voice of the Spirit at the local level. It happens in some parishes because there's a common and prayerful understanding of the theology of the church. It happens in others because the parishioners (or a critical mass of parishioners) have insisted on it based on their understanding of the theology of the laity. Some pastors too extend a kind of servant openness, not just to the councils but to the parish as a whole, since they are alert to the sense of the faithful in the local community. I am reminded of a pastor who was told by his bishop to require Sunday Mass worshipers to cease standing during the Eucharistic prayer and kneel instead. The pastor replied, "I'll tell them but I don't think they'll do it."

Psychologist Eugene Kennedy has described the condition of modern Catholicism in terms of two distinct cultures, Culture One Catholics are those for whom the church as institution is an all-embracing "spine and central nervous system."[1] They may love the system or deeply resent it, but they are preoccupied with "control" as the critical dynamic of faith. In one way or other, they are still under the spell of the Grand Inquisitor. Culture Two Catholics, according to Kennedy, see the church essentially as mystery and find it "far less institutionally compelling" than do Culture One members. They have become "psychologically independent of the canonically erected, clerically layered, historically envisaged church"[2] that is proclaimed, for example, by the Eternal Word Television Network or Catholic Relevant Radio stations. Culture Two members "do not reject episcopal authority, but they certainly do not accept official pronouncements automatically anymore." Culture Two thinking is at work in those priests, laity, and parishes which operate collegially and democratically today, while regarding canonical restrictions as interesting but not determinative in every instance. This, I believe, is the future of Catholicism.

At this point, the vast majority of bishops and pastors still operate in accord with the relevant canons. And in some places the congregation is happy to have it that way — father knows best. Still, there are rumblings from below: bishops deeply resentful that their national conferences can make virtually no decision without Vatican approval, pastors who wilt under the load of responsibility that is theirs alone, facing a passive council which routinely rubber-stamps the pastor's decisions since they have no authority and know it. This is not the future of Catholicism.

There are, however, indications that the Vatican fears Culture Two Catholicism because of its relativistic tendencies. Members of reform groups I spoke with foresee a deliberate push for a smaller, purer Catholicism in the years ahead. "From reading Cardinal Ratzinger's work," said Rea Howarth, "I get the impression that's where we're heading." The absolute refusal to even discuss controversial teaching, the willingness to close Catholic schools and parishes, the selling of real estate holdings — all point "to a period of purification, the era of the faithful remnant," she said. Author Peter Steinfels expressed a similar concern in discussing the Vatican's reaction to the abuse scandal.

> The poisonous root of the scandal, it is declared, is the "culture of dissent," primarily, that is, the rejection by many laypeople, clergy and theologians of *Humanae Vitae*. The remedy is certainly not consultation and dialogue, therefore, but the reassertion of authority, especially papal authority, and the rooting out of church roles of all who do not publicly and unquestioningly identify themselves with it. This vision of exercising leadership talks of "purification," but what it seems to mean is "purge."[3]

Pope Benedict XVI himself has proposed on several occasions a "smaller, more faithful" church as an antidote to modern culture.

If such a purification campaign is mounted, it will rely for success on the authority of the Culture One bishops appointed in the past thirty years, the considerable presence of young, Culture One priests emerging from conservative seminaries, and the importing of Culture One clergy from foreign countries. However, a purge can work only if people will leave the premises when told to go. I believe the self-understanding and the theological maturity of laity and clergy will soldier through misguided attempts to separate the sheep from the goats. Already the number of house churches, small faith groups, and alternative Catholic communities is larger than the institution realizes, and the presence of ordained women priests and bishops discussed in chapter 12 may provide an interesting dynamic in hard times. The trajectory toward democratization will not be stalled for long. In Kennedy's view:

> Ultimately pragmatic, the organization will eventually and inevitably make peace with its own people, emphasizing and implementing rather than insisting on a progressively less efficacious authoritarian style. In other words, the Catholic Church will, in the future, form itself increasingly around a Culture Two consciousness in order to survive and grow organically. The old arguments and seemingly deathless causes of Culture One — celibacy and the other death rattles of authoritarianism — will cease to be relevant and will, as a result, drop away naturally.[4]

When peace is made, author Paul Lakeland suggests what the church might look like at the parish level. The troubling distinction between laity and clergy having passed into disuse, the parish will be led by a small team of ministers, all of whom have been chosen by the people and subsequently ordained by the bishop to celebrate the Eucharist, though this may not be their major contribution. They will have training in theology and Scripture studies. In addition the parish will have a substantial number of ministers serving within the community in areas like music, youth, caring for the sick, social justice, etc., some part-time, some full-time. What binds them together, says Lakeland, "is that all, paid or volunteer, understand their work for the church as ministry rather than employment, and the community recognizes this too." The third and largest group consists of those who work in the secular sphere and are best considered as "ministers to the world." All three of these groups are responsible for the governance of the community. The elected parish council will have representation from all three groups, and its decisions will be deliberative and binding. In this new configuration, Lakeland explains, there is no "cultic separation" between those ordained to preside and those with other ministries, and there are no restrictions in any of the roles based on gender or commitment to celibacy. Changes such as these, he says, will clearly signal the end of "the infantilization of the laity."[5]

Reworking Papal Primacy

Scenario 2: A reconsideration and redefinition of the primacy of the pope would be a powerful step in the direction of democratization and send reverberations around the world. Such a move may not be far off. Pope John Paul II's 1995 encyclical *Ut Unum Sint,* discussed in chapter 11, awakened long-simmering ideas about Christian unity, and speculation about its possible implementation continues. John Paul said, in effect, that his primacy, that is, the ancient belief in the pope's supreme jurisdiction over the church and the duty of all Christians to obey him as head of the universal church, is the leading obstacle to the unity of believers that Christ prayed for. He asked for help in healing the break and said it was especially necessary that he find a "new way" to exercise his primacy in view of "the new situation." What he meant by "new situation" was not entirely clear. What was clear was his sense of urgency about taking productive, ecumenical steps toward unity.

Rejection of primacy was a major reason for the split between the Eastern Orthodox churches and Rome in the eleventh century. It was also a prime factor in the Protestant split in the sixteenth century. Despite the gentle words of Vatican II concerning the ability of non-Catholic churches to "engender a life of grace" and provide "access to the community of salvation," the split remains. The rift weighed heavily on John Paul, and his successor, Benedict XVI, was quick to list among his priorities ecumenical efforts, especially with the Orthodox churches. So it is not a stretch to suggest that he or a pope to come in the near future would decide to go well beyond speeches and short, friendly, photo-op meetings with the separated sisters and brothers.

The process might begin with a series of discussions between the pope and theologians, canonists, historians, ecumenists, and liturgists to determine what concessions he could make without compromising the faith. He and a board of experts would then enter into a series of intense dialogues with top representatives from other Christian churches and denominations. The intent would be to move forward gradually while refraining from (as John Paul suggested) getting bogged down in "useless controversies." Talks of this magnitude would probably continue over weeks and months. And the prolonged engagement would surely sensitize participants to the problems and priorities of the involved churches and provide new awareness of what constitutes faithfulness to the gospel message.

What would the pope be willing to yield in terms of his primacy in order to promote formal unification? What changes would Protestant and Orthodox churches require in order to acknowledge the papal position, and what would they be willing to yield on their part? Formally downgrading primacy in any way would be seen as a stupendous step, a kind of emptying of himself of those attitudes and titles that have rankled and offended many Christians for centuries.

Since I am not likely to be in the papal negotiating party, I feel free to suggest some preparatory changes the pope might consider to make primacy more acceptable to the separated brothers and sisters. He could drastically tone down the amount of sheer pageantry and triumphalism associated with papal ceremonies, audiences, and his travels around the world. He could terminate the college of cardinals in favor of a broader, more representative group to elect the pope. He could retire meaningless titles like "monsignor" and embarrassing honorifics like "your excellency," "your eminence," and certainly "your holiness." He could restrict the title of "bishop" only to the person who is in charge of an existing diocese, and he could require that bishops be elected by the people and priests of the dioceses they will serve. He could demonstrate his collegial, open approach in the way he interacts with his fellow bishops. None of this would imperil sacred doctrine. It would instead signal that the pope does not intend to "lord it over" his colleagues in ministry. It would indicate to all that he is taking very seriously his most important title, "servant of the servants of the Lord."

Down the line, the pope would have to reinterpret his understanding of primacy itself as something less than "immediate jurisdiction" over all the baptized in the world. The function of the papacy might be recast (as John Paul suggested in his encyclical) as that of "keeping watch" over the Christian world or just maintaining "vigilance." He could serve as advisor to the newly unified churches, as they maintain many of their own traditions and charisms. As the process goes on, constant explanation of what is happening and full communication with the public would be vitally important, Steps toward unity would have to be tested and modeled among the rank-and-file faithful of all the participating denominations, and final decisions would necessarily require approval at these levels too. In other words, finding a "new way" will be a decidedly democratic process, a process that would have ramifications from top to bottom in Catholicism and other Christian churches for centuries to come.

Taking the Mission Seriously

Scenario 3: Something fascinating would occur if the Catholic Church should decide as a whole to alter its priorities and take its mission very seriously — that is, to take responsibility for showing what the reign of God is about rather than talking about it. This is something the Asian bishops have been working to achieve on their continent for the last thirty years, as discussed in chapter 11. It is opening the Asian church to the larger world and creating an active participatory community. An essential component of the plan is carrying on dialogue with other faiths, with culture, and with the poor.

Within this approach, the church ceases to be the center around which all activity revolves, while organized effort to relieve suffering, aid the poor, reduce violence and tension, and build responsible, stable communities wherever they are needed becomes the primary goal. In other words, the beatitudes are placed ahead of everything else. It is true that the church, through its agencies, has promoted works of charity and still does so on a substantial basis. But what if the full wealth and energy of Catholicism were directed toward a serious intervention in the world situation in this century — a world in which 10 percent of the population controls 85 percent of the global wealth and 90 percent of the population struggles to survive on 15 percent of the wealth?

Catholics are generally aware of this growing inequity. The pope and bishops talk about it often, and ordinary parishioners often do something to help, realizing their contribution is only a drop in the bucket and hardly impinges on their own lifestyle. To shake us all out of acceptance of the rich-poor imbalance, it might take a major catastrophe, like a truly devastating earthquake or an especially horrific famine or an obliterating genocidal war — or even a nuclear incident. None of these tragic occurrences is beyond the realm of possibility, especially the possibility of a nuclear attack, within the foreseeable future. Of course, it should not require an immense new tragedy to summon a dedication to mission. The regular starvation deaths of hundreds of thousands in Africa is tragedy enough. The push would have to come from below and from above — lay groups lobbying for a change in priorities and the pope announcing this historic shift and calling on the cooperation of the universal church. If it were to take as its mission a full, extended commitment to the blind, the lame, the homeless, and the hopeless, then a series of corollaries would follow.

First, the laity would have to lead, since it is the laity, not the clergy, who operate in the secular sphere and understand the what, where, how, and when of developing strategies and applying the necessary resources.

Second, since the church would be working in solidarity with other organizations, religious and secular, it would necessarily have to moderate or abandon for practical purposes some of its idiosyncratic practices. Commenting on commitment, author Paul Lakeland said it would be impossible for a church "still locked in a rigidly hierarchical framework" to say anything convincing to the secular world or to cooperate on an equal basis: "A church that seems so often to prize secrecy over accountability and that maintains a pre-modern attitude toward women... cannot carry conviction when it talks the language of human solidarity. If rights are to be promoted, the community that promotes them had better have evidence that it lives by them."[6]

Third, the church would have to come to terms with modernity in a practical way. On the one hand, it is well equipped to critique capitalism as a way of being that divinizes acquisition and privileges greed. On the other hand, it would have to acknowledge that modernity had raised the potential for self-realization and a flourishing of life far beyond what was possible in earlier eras. Dedication to mission and ongoing dialogue would force the church to admit it does not have all the answers, that it has much to learn from modernity, and that harangues against modernity's abuses are usually counterproductive.

Does this mean a mission-oriented Catholicism must simply throw in its lot with every altruistic, humanistic operation in the world? I do not think so. In all it does, the church, by its nature, has a transcendent vision — a belief in something more than natural life. In fact, it's that vision that impels efforts to make the world achieve its potential or to come closer, in gospel terms, to the kingdom of God. A church community so oriented might even inspire others to inquire out of what wellspring that energy comes. But the operative goal here is not to gain converts but to love the neighbor by doing the works of mercy and overcoming the dehumanizing factors operating in society. The Asian bishops and people remain committed to the task. It would be quite remarkable if the church in a continent that is about 1 percent Catholic should lead the way in radically transforming the full church — and democratizing it in the process. Yet paradox and surprise are deeply rooted in Christian tradition.

The End of Celibate and Male Exclusivity

Scenario 4: A simple change in church discipline, which has long been a subject of hot discussion and which is supported by many, could become the catalyst for forming the democratic church. It is the removal of the obligation of lifelong celibacy for Catholic clergy. Pressure on the Vatican to rescind the requirement is based on theological, psychological, and pragmatic reasons. At present the pragmatic argument is the most persuasive. There are not enough priests to supply the needs of the Catholic community in the United States and elsewhere. And the situation is only going to get worse, making the Eucharist less and less available to the faithful. Put bluntly, church authority is going to have to choose between Eucharist and the rule of celibacy.

Allowing married clergy would not, of itself, create a democratic church. Its first benefit would be a larger supply of priests and seminarians and quick reduction in the need for priest-less Sunday services and circuit-riding pastors. Studies consistently show church law requiring the celibate commitment to be the major reason young people (and older too) are not attracted to the priesthood.

The law could be abrogated with a simple announcement from the Vatican. In fact, the public is well prepared for that announcement, since the U.S. church in the past twenty years has been accepting into the priesthood Protestant ministers and Episcopalian priests who convert to Catholicism, bringing with them their wives and children and sometimes their whole congregations. Clergy, including many popes, were married during the first millennium. So there are no doctrinal or historical roadblocks to the proposed change.

It will do more than introduce women and children into the rectory. It will bring a distinctive female contribution into the lives of priests and, by extension, into parish ministry, and it is bound to have a devastating effect on the worst aspects of clericalism. Besides that, and more importantly, it will open the way for the ordination of women.

The late sociologist Richard Schoenherr spent twenty-five years of his professional life analyzing American priests. In his first book, *Full Pews and Empty Altars*, he discussed the how and why of the priest drain and provided precise estimates diocese by diocese of the number of active priests well into the current century — estimates which have proven to be amazingly accurate. In his second book, *Goodbye Father: The Celibate Male Priesthood and the Future of the Catholic Church*, Schoenherr charged that the church remains stubbornly opposed to a married clergy because "it constitutes the camel's nose under the patriarchal tent."[7]

Patriarchy, he argues, is the real villain, crippling the church and stifling the liberating message of the gospel. He cites the works of feminist scholars like Gerda Lerner, who "are uncovering the ignorance of the old patriarchal paradigm, exposing the insidious history and nature of patriarchy, its sedimented massiveness, its horrible destructiveness of women's equality, freedom and dignity."[8] In insisting on an exclusively male and exclusively celibate priesthood, he contends, the church has prevented Catholics from seeing clearly the ugly head of patriarchy. Celibacy by itself has a certain sacred character since it is presumably chosen freely out of selfless religious motives. Gender of itself does not have that character because it is not chosen; it is what one is born with. Therefore, when the two exclusives are joined, as they are in Roman Catholic law, exclusive celibacy acts to mask with an aura of holiness the nakedness of exclusive maleness. Says Schoenherr, "Male exclusivity and celibate exclusivity reinforce one another. Letting go of celibate exclusivity would expose male exclusivity in the priesthood for what it is: a historically developed form of gender dominance. If celibate exclusivity is recognized as theologically and pastorally outmoded, then male exclusivity can be subjected to similar criticism, found wanting, and be rejected as well."[9]

All indicators point to the elimination of celibacy as a priesthood obligation. When this happens, speculates Schoenherr, pressure for women's ordination may lessen for a time because of the availability of more male priests serving the Catholic community. But the pressure will return in a stronger, more aggressive form when male exclusivity is clearly seen as an open manifestation of patriarchy, preventing full and equal participation by half the members of the church. The acceptance of women into the priesthood will inevitably provoke a reconsideration of all the other manifestations of patriarchy in the church and perhaps in society as well. It will herald the coming of democratization. As some observers have noted, the extension of the priesthood to women could well be the greatest step forward in the church since the apostles and disciples in first-century Jerusalem broke with tradition and threw open the doors to the Gentiles.

It Will Surely Come!

Of course there are other possible scenarios. A general council of the church that was truly ecumenical, that is, one that included not just Catholics, but also gave voice to the Eastern Orthodox churches, the Protestant churches, and the lay presence as well, could work wonders. This council would have to be organized by a broad commission of competent and holy leaders from around the world. It should not be held in the Vatican but somewhere else, perhaps in São Paulo, Lagos, Manila, or another city where the church of the future is aborning, and it would require a holy and audacious leader to show the way. Fortunately, the memory of Pope John XXIII is still alive and well.

Full participation could occur if American Catholicism were to become a separate rite in full communion with the full church. It would be a so-called autochthonous church, "modeled on the ancient Churches of the Middle East — the Chaldeans, the Maronites, the Melkites, the Armenians, and the Copts, for example, who are Catholics united with Rome, with their own patriarchs, their own liturgies, and their mostly married clergy."[10] Calls for such a relationship have been voiced as recently as 2001 by the Indonesian bishops' conference in an effort to free their dioceses themselves from Vatican extreme centralization.

Or it could conceivably come if a great mass of U.S. Catholics — or Catholics worldwide — were to become so disillusioned and disgusted as to withhold all contributions to the church. There has been talk of such a move for years, and, in the wake of the clergy sexual abuse scandal, many dioceses and parishes saw their income from Sunday worship and special collections plummet precipitously for a time. Refusing to give is an extremely direct way to signal no confidence in leadership and is almost guaranteed to get the attention of the hierarchy. A well-organized and clearly targeted campaign of non-giving might well prove a last resort if there is no good-faith resolution to the present crises.

I began these considerations with my musings on Dostoyevsky's Grand Inquisitor. I was fascinated with this figure who served a God he did not believe in, who felt sorry for poor, sinful humanity, and who believed people would be happier and more content in submitting blindly to control by him and his church. I caught more than a few glimpses of the Grand Inquisitor Syndrome in some of the church leaders I encountered in history, in some I've met since, and in some who are still around. But the price for such control has always been too high. It has robbed Christians of their most precious possession and given leaders the sense that they are God instead of the servants of God. Now the recovery of freedom, participation, openness, and democracy is under way; the church, I am convinced, is moving back toward what it was meant to be and inexorably forward into the reign of God.

Meanwhile, I love the wisdom of the prophets of Israel, like Habakkuk: "The vision still has its time, presses on to fulfillment, and will not disappoint," he says. "If it delays, wait for it. It will surely come, it will not be late" (2:3, NAB).

Notes

------- ✝ -------

Introduction

1. Except where noted, quotes in this chapter are from Fyodor Dostoyevsky, *The Brothers Karamazov* (New York: Modern Library, 1950), 292–314.

2. Pope Pius X, "Oath Against Modernism," Catholic Information Network, website.

Chapter 1: The Community Jesus Founded

1. All Scripture citations in this chapter are from *The Bible: New Revised Standard Version* (New York: Oxford University Press, 1990).

2. Stephen L. Harris, *The New Testament: A Student's Edition* (Boston: McGraw Hill, 2002), 304.

3. Ibid., 321.

4. Raymond E. Brown, S.S., *The Churches the Apostles Left Behind* (New York: Paulist Press, 1984), 35.

5. Ibid., 38.

6. Ibid., 45.

7. Cited in Harris, *The New Testament: A Student's Edition*, 370.

8. Cited in Gregory Dix and Henry Chadwick, eds., *Treatise on the Apostolic Tradition of St. Hippolytus of Rome, Bishop and Martyr* (Ridgefield, Conn.: Morehouse Publishing, 1991), 2–3.

9. Luke Timothy Johnson, *The Acts of the Apostles*, Sacra Pagina Series 5 (Collegeville, Minn.: Liturgical Press, 1992), 261.

10. Ibid., 279.

11. Ibid., 271.

12. Luke Timothy Johnson, *Scriptural Discernment: Decision Making in the Church* (Nashville: Abingdon Press, 1983), 142.

13. Ibid., 151.

Chapter 2: A Man for All Seasons

1. Quotations in this section are from Francine Cardman, "Myth, History and the Beginnings of the Church," in *Governance, Accountability,*

and the Future of the Catholic Church, ed. Francis Oakley and Bruce Russett (New York: Continuum, 2004), 34–40.

2. *The Letters of St. Cyprian of Carthage, Bishop and Martyr,* trans. G. W. Clarke (New York: Newman Press, 1984), 3:62.

3. Ibid., 1:72.

4. Ibid., 2:55.

5. Ibid., 1:88.

6. Ibid., 3:97.

7. Ibid., 1:93.

8. Ibid., 3:70.

9. Ibid., 1:19.

10. Ibid., 1:89. Italicized quotes in this section are by author.

11. Ibid., 1:97.

12. Ibid., 2:52.

13. Ibid., 4:23.

14. Ibid.

15. Ibid., 3:83–84.

16. Ibid., 2:77–79.

17. Francis Sullivan, S.J., "St. Cyprian on the Role of the Laity in Decision Making in the Early Church," in *Common Calling: The Laity and Governance of the Catholic Church,* ed. Stephen J. Pope (Washington, D.C.: Georgetown University Press, 2004), 48.

18. Michael J. Buckley, S.J., "Resources for Reform from the First Millennium," *Common Calling,* 73.

Chapter 3: A Rising Up of the Faithful

1. Newman's summary of synods and councils after Nicaea is found in John H. Newman, *On Consulting the Faithful in Matters of Doctrine* (Kansas City, Mo.: Sheed and Ward, 1961), 77–82.

2. For the reaction of Pro-Nicaeans see ibid., 84–85.

3. For a summary of resistance see ibid., 86–100.

4. Cited in Francine Cardman, "Laity and the Development of Doctrine: Perspectives from the Early Church," in *Common Calling: The Laity and Governance of the Catholic Church,* ed. Stephen J. Pope (Washington, D.C., Georgetown University Press, 2004), 63–64.

5. John Coulson, Introduction to *On Consulting the Faithful,* 13.

6. Newman, *On Consulting the Faithful,* 77.

7. Ibid., 75.

8. Ibid., 63.

Chapter 4: Control from Above, Participation from Below

1. Brian Tierney, "Church Law and Alternative Structures," in *Governance, Accountability, and the Future of the Catholic Church*, ed. Francis Oakley and Bruce Russett (New York: Continuum, 2004), 51.

2. This and the following quotes cited in Marcia Colish, "Reclaiming Our History: Belief and Practice in the Church," in *Governance, Accountability, and the Future of the Catholic Church*, 65.

3. Cited in William J. La Due, *The Chair of St. Peter: A History of the Papacy* (Maryknoll, N.Y.: Orbis Books, 1999), 67.

4. Cited in Tierney, in *Governance, Accountability, and the Future of the Catholic Church*, 55.

5. Cited in "Reclaiming Our History," 66.

6. La Due, *The Chair of St. Peter*, 67.

7. Ibid., 98.

8. Cited in Thomas Bokenkotter, *A Concise History of the Catholic Church* (New York: Doubleday, 1990), 103.

9. Ibid., 105.

10. Cited in La Due, *The Chair of St. Peter*, 102.

11. Ibid., 100.

12. Cited in Bokenkotter, *A Concise History of the Catholic Church*, 107.

13. Cited in Tierney, in *Governance, Accountability, and the Future of the Catholic Church*, 50.

14. Cited in Bokenkotter, *A Concise History of the Catholic Church*, 160.

15. Cited in Brian Tierney, *Religion, Law, and the Growth of Constitutional Thought* (London: Cambridge University Press, 1982), 14.

16. Ibid., 27.

17. Ibid., 58.

18. Ibid., 61.

Chapter 5: Conciliarism

1. George Orwell, *1984* (New York: Signet Classics, 1950), 80.

2. Francis Oakley, *Council over Pope: Towards a Provisional Ecclesiology* (New York: Herder and Herder, 1969), 68.

3. Cited in Thomas Bokenkotter, *A Concise History of the Catholic Church* (New York: Doubleday, 1990), 170.

4. Oakley, *Council over Pope*, 75.

5. Ibid., 73.

6. William J. La Due, *The Chair of St. Peter: A History of the Papacy* (Maryknoll, N.Y.: Orbis Books, 1999), 308.

7. Francis A. Sullivan, *Magisterium: Teaching Authority in the Catholic Church* (New York: Paulist Press, 1984), 74.

8. Oakley, *Council over Pope*, 74.

Chapter 6: The American Experiment in Democracy

1. Jay Dolan, "The Desire for Democracy in the American Catholic Church," in *A Democratic Catholic Church* (New York: Crossroad, 1992), 114.

2. Cited in Robert J. Willis, *The Democracy of God: An American Catholicism* (New York: iUniverse, 2006), 20.

3. Ibid., 21.

4. Ibid., 22.

5. Cited in Jay Dolan, *The American Catholic Experience: A History from Colonial Times to the Present* (New York: Doubleday, 1985), 105.

6. Dolan, *A Democratic Catholic Church*, 117.

7. Cited in Willis, *The Democracy of God*, 25.

8. Cited in Dolan, *The American Catholic Experience*, 112.

9. Ibid., 113.

10. Cited in Willis, *The Democracy of God*, 31–32.

11. Cited in Gerald P. Fogarty, S.J., "Episcopal Governance in the American Church," in *Governance, Accountability, and the Future of the Catholic Church*, ed. Francis Oakley and Bruce Russett (New York: Continuum, 2004), 105.

12. Ibid., 106.

13. Dolan, *A Democratic Catholic Church*, 123.

Chapter 7: The Emergence of the Laity

1. Quotes in the section above are from Paul Lakeland, *The Liberation of the Laity: In Search of an Accountable Church* (New York: Continuum, 2003), 55–61.

2. "Dogmatic Decree on the Constitution of the Church," nos. 10–11, *The Documents of Vatican II* (New York: America Press, 1966).

3. Ibid., no. 12.

4. Ibid., no. 33.

5. Ibid., no. 34.

6. Ibid., no. 37.

7. "Decree on the Apostolate of the Laity," no. 7, *The Documents of Vatican II*.

8. Ibid., nos. 2–3.

9. Cited in Lakeland, *The Liberation of the Laity*, 216.

10. Cited in Thomas Bokenkotter, *A Concise History of the Catholic Church* (New York: Doubleday, 1990), 335.

11. Lakeland, *The Liberation of the Laity*, 216.

12. Ladislas Orsy, *The Church Learning and Teaching* (Wilmington, Del.: Michael Glazier, 1987), 42.

13. David Gibson, *The Coming Catholic Church: How the Faithful Are Shaping a New American Catholicism* (New York: HarperSanFrancisco, 2003), 57.

14. Cited in Lakeland, *The Liberation of the Laity*, 128.

15. Alice Camille, "Laity on the Line," *U.S. Catholic*, July 7, 2002.

Chapter 8: Learning to Live With Democracy

1. Quotes in this section are from Peter Steinfels, "Necessary but Not Sufficient: A Response to Bishop Wuerl's Reflection," in *Governance, Accountability, and the Future of the Catholic Church*, ed. Francis Oakley and Bruce Russett (New York: Continuum, 2004), 16–28.

2. Cited in William J. La Due, *The Chair of St. Peter: A History of the Papacy* (Maryknoll, N.Y.: Orbis Books, 1999), 237.

3. Paul Lakeland, *The Liberation of the Laity: In Search of an Accountable Church* (New York: Continuum, 2003), 156.

4. Thomas Bokenkotter, *A Concise History of the Catholic Church* (New York: Doubleday, 1990), 303.

5. The Pastoral Constitution of the Church, no. 1, *The Documents of Vatican II* (New York: America Press, 1966).

6. Ibid., no. 44.

7. John Beal, "It Shall Not Be So among You," in *Governance, Accountability, and the Future of the Catholic Church*, 98.

8. James E. Muller and Charles Kenney, *Keep the Faith, Change the Church* (New York: Rodale, 2004), 83.

9. Terence L. Nichols, *That All May Be One: Hierarchy and Participation in the Church* (Collegeville, Minn.: Liturgical Press, 1997), 289.

10. Ibid., 291.

11. Ibid., 292.

12. Cited in ibid., 293.

13. Jim Mateja, "Farewell Taurus," *Chicago Tribune*, November 25, 2006. Ford is bringing the Taurus brand back for the 2008 model year.

14. Nichols, *That All May Be One*, 299.

15. Pope John Paul II, "Address to the Pontifical Society of the Social Sciences," February 24, 2000, Vatican website.

16. Nichols, *That All May Be One*, 299.

17. Cited in ibid., 302.

Chapter 9: The Church as a Democracy

1. Francis A. Sullivan, *Magisterium: Teaching Authority in the Church* (New York: Paulist Press, 1983), 15.
2. Ibid., 31.
3. Ibid., 32.
4. John H. Newman, *On Consulting the Faithful in Matters of Doctrine* (Kansas City, Mo.: Sheed and Ward, 1961), 63.
5. Sullivan, *Magisterium*, 104.
6. Ibid., 111
7. Ibid., 115.
8. "Decree on Ecumenism, no. 3," *The Documents of Vatican II* (New York: America Press, 1966).
9. Sullivan, *Magisterium*, 180.
10. Cited in Patrick Granfield, *The Limits of the Papacy: Authority and Autonomy in the Church* (New York: Crossroad, 1987), 150.
11. Sullivan, *Magisterium*, 106.
12. Ibid., 118.
13. Ibid., 165.
14. Ibid., 166.

Chapter 10: A Convergence of Crises

1. Richard Schoenherr, Lawrence Young, and Tsan-Yuanf Cheng, *Full Pews and Empty Altars* (Madison: University of Wisconsin Press, 1993), 25–48.
2. Kenneth Briggs, *Double Crossed: Uncovering the Catholic Church's Betrayal of American Nuns* (New York: Doubleday, 2006), 118.
3. Ibid., 121.
4. Richard McBrien, "Dialogue in the Church," *Essays in Theology,* Syndicated column, September 11, 2006.
5. Dean Hoge, "Center of Catholic Identity," *National Catholic Reporter,* September 30, 2005.
6. David Gibson, *The Coming Catholic Church: How the Faithful Are Shaping a New American Catholicism* (New York: HarperSanFrancisco, 2003), 66.
7. Cited in ibid., 77–79.
8. Deborah Halter, "Journey in Faith," *National Catholic Reporter,* September 1, 2006.
9. Genevieve O'Hara, "Why I Won't Stay," *National Catholic Reporter,* March 9, 2001.
10. Paige Byrne Shortal, "For Women — and Men," *National Catholic Reporter,* February 23, 2001.

11. Jeannette Batz, "Women Finding Ways," *National Catholic Reporter*, March 9, 2001.

12. Margaret Murphy, "Women's Priesthood? Few Women Agree," *National Catholic Reporter*, January 1, 1997.

13. Rosemary Radford Ruether, *Women-Church: Theology and Practice* (San Francisco: Harper & Row, 1986), 4.

14. Gerard Mannion, "A Haze of Fiction: Legitimacy, Accountability and Truthfulness," in *Governance, Accountability, and the Future of the Catholic Church*, ed. Francis Oakley and Bruce Russett (New York: Continuum, 2004), 162.

15. Steinfels, "Necessary but Not Sufficient: A Response to Bishop Wuerl's Reflection," in *Governance, Accountability, and the Future of the Catholic Church*, 26.

Chapter 11: Reform from Above

1. John R. Quinn, *The Reform of the Papacy: The Costly Call to Christian Unity* (New York: Crossroad, 1999), 34.

2. Decree on Ecumenism, no. 3, *Documents of Vatican II* (New York: America Press, 1966).

3. Pope John Paul II, encyclical *Ut Unum Sint*, Vatican website, no. 98.

4. Ibid., no. 9.

5. Ibid., no. 95.

6. Ibid., no. 96.

7. Ibid., no. 95.

8. Thomas C. Fox, *Pentecost in Asia: A New Way of Being Church* (Maryknoll, N.Y.: Orbis Books, 2002), 10.

9. Ibid., 30

10. Ibid., 20.

11. Peter C. Phan, "A New Way of Being Church: Perspectives from Asia," in *Governance, Accountability, and the Future of the Catholic Church*, ed. Francis Oakley and Bruce Russett (New York: Continuum, 2004), 183.

12. Ibid., 186.

13. Fox, *Pentecost in Asia*, 75.

14. Ibid., 167.

15. Ibid., 178.

16. Cited in Robert McClory, "Will Catholics Be Lonely in Heaven?" *U.S. Catholic*, September 2001.

17. Dennis P. McCann, *New Experiment in Democracy: The Challenge for American Catholicism* (Kansas City, Mo.: Sheed & Ward, 1987), 42.

18. Cited in Margery Frisbie, *An Alley in Chicago: The Ministry of a City Priest* (Kansas City, Mo.: Sheed & Ward, 1991), 259.

19. McCann, *New Experiment in Democracy,* 46.

20. Cited in ibid., 48–49.

21. David O'Brien, interview with author, November 4, 2006.

Chapter 12: Pressure from Below

1. James E. Muller, *Keep the Faith, Change the Church* (New York: Rodale, 2004), 83.

2. Cited in ibid., 109.

3. Cited in ibid., 161.

4. Cited in ibid., 165.

5. Cited in David Gibson, *The Coming Catholic Church: How the Faithful Are Shaping a New American Catholicism* (New York: Harper-SanFrancisco, 2003), 131.

6. Ibid., 175.

7. Cited in ibid., 258.

8. Anthony Padovano, "To What Have We Been Committed?" *Corpus Reports* 32, no. 5 (September–October 2006): 26.

9. Patricia Fresen, "Prophetic Disobedience: The Experience and Vision of Roman Catholic WomenPriests," *Roman Catholic WomenPriests* website.

10. Rea Howarth, interview with author, December 27, 2006.

11. William Thompson, interview with author, January 3, 2007.

Chapter 13: The Vision Presses On to Fulfillment

1. Eugene Kennedy, *Tomorrow's Catholic, Yesterday's Church: The Two Cultures of American Catholicism* (New York: Harper & Row Publishers, 1988), 21.

2. Ibid., 18.

3. Peter Steinfels, *A People Adrift: The Crisis of the Roman Catholic Church in America* (New York: Simon & Schuster, 2005), 353.

4. Kennedy, *Tomorrow's Catholic, Yesterday's Church,* 33.

5. Paul Lakeland, *The Liberation of the Laity: In Search of an Accountable Church* (New York: Continuum, 2003), 270.

6. Ibid., 230.

7. Richard Schoenherr, *Goodbye Father: The Celibate Male Priesthood and the Future of the Catholic Church* (New York: Oxford University Press, 2005) 205.

8. Ibid., 211.

9. Ibid., 205.

10. Robert Blair Kaiser, *A Church in Search of Itself: Benedict XVI and the Battle for the Future* (New York: Alfred A. Knopf, 2006), 243.

Index

✝

Also by Robert McClory

TURNING POINT

*The Inside Story
of the Papal Birth Control Commission,
and How Humanae Vitae Changed the Life
of Patty Crowley and the Future of the Church*

Historians agree that the Vatican decision to go
against the majority report of the Papal Birth Control
Commission is one of the most important events in
Catholic history in the twentieth century. To many, the
encyclical *Humanae Vitae* represents both a turning
point and a lost moment. Award-winning journalist
Robert McClory brings to life the incredible events
surrounding that decision, and reveals its meaning in
a way that will stick in memory, stir new debate, and
impact the future.

0-8245-1613-3, paperback

Check your local bookstore for availability.
To order directly from the publisher,
please call 1-800-707-0670 for Customer Service
or visit our Web site at *www.cpcbooks.com.*
For catalog orders, please send your request to the address below.

THE CROSSROAD PUBLISHING COMPANY
16 Penn Plaza, Suite 1550
New York, NY 10001

crossroad